How to Get
20 to 90% Off
on Everything You Buy

How to Get

20 to 90% Off

on Everything You Buy

Jean and Cle Kinney

Parker Publishing Company, Inc.

WEST NYACK

NEW YORK

PRINTED IN THE UNITED STATES OF AMERICA

40975—B&P

Human felicity is produced not so much by great pieces of good fortune that seldom happen —as by little advantages that occur every day.

Benjamin Franklin

How This Book Can Help You

Only you know why you opened this book. But chances are it is for one of these five reasons.

1. You have an excellent income, but you have a nagging feeling that you are spending more than you should be spending for your daily needs. If you can satisfy your present requirements with less money, you will have more to invest for the future when your income may be less.

2. You are living on a set income planned for long ago in a pension plan or through an annuity purchase. Inflation has minimized the buying power of your dollar. The only way for you to live better is to find a way to get more for your money.

3. You are facing a financial emergency of some kind. You may be temporarily unemployed, or a severe illness may be depleting your resources, or you may have one or more children in college. Your problem is to meet your present emergency without going deep into debt.

4. Your income is bound to go up. Your only trouble is that your tastes run to what you won't be able to afford, you think, until five years from now. *What you are looking for is a way to buy what you want now.*

5. You want to get out of the "rat race," but you need every cent you are making to keep up with your daily needs. Perhaps if you can find a way to live for less, you can consider another type of work or another way of life.

In any case, your desire is to live as well as you are now living (or even better) for less than you are now spending.

This aim is not new to man.

"An economist," Ralph Waldo Emerson wrote 100 years ago,

"is a man who can bring the year round with expenditure which expresses his character without embarrassing one day of his future." In his essay on Wealth he defined such a person as one who is "already a master of life and a free man." This book will help you get what you want without embarrassment. The method? To expand the buying power of every dollar you have to spend.

More buying power per dollar

Price cuts here are for those who enjoy spending but who do not have the dollars to buy all they want.

In less than 15 years, the purchasing power of our dollar has decreased 20%. To live as people lived a few years ago for the same outlay, you must buy for 20% off the regular price. So that is the goal of this book. *At least 20% off!* Some savings are for 90%, but the average price cut here is 30%. Get 30% off on everything you buy, and you will live better than others making 20% more. Simple arithmetic, but few approach everyday economics this way.

As an average American you spend money in one of three ways. (1) You scrimp on pleasures you know should be yours. (2) You go the other way; you over-spend, telling yourself that your present state cannot be permanent. Or (3) you swing violently from one extreme to the other. By far the largest number of Americans spend their lives in the number-two camp. Paycheck after paycheck, they turn their money over to creditors, appeasing themselves with the thought that some day, some way, there will be "more."

The fallacy of "more"

You are an unusual person if you have never told yourself, "Everything will be all right if I can just get a raise." Or "I'll get everything paid for if that stock I bought goes up." Or "Maybe, I'll inherit some money sometime." These thoughts are pacifiers.

The truth is that once you are caught up in a rush for more money, and more and more and more, your quest for better living just *has* to fail. Here's why: (1) Prices go up as salaries go up, so unless your raise is a very important one, you will have very little more buying power than you have now. Inherited money may provide a higher fixed income, but the prices of what you want will not be fixed. They will continue to go up. (2) Your wants will increase as your taste improves. Once you own a fine painting, the department store prints you got for a wedding present will seem bland. One handsomely tailored suit will make you feel uncomfortable in all suits that don't have the same "hand" and fit and feel. One small lustrous end table will make a borax table look shoddy. (3) As your small business ventures pay off, you will be pulled into bigger investments. Achieve one dream and you will immediately pursue another. If you overspend to attain each dream, your desires will become insatiable.

Read the italicized words which comprise the next paragraph. Then, put a bookmark there. Before you begin the main body of this book, return and read the words again. This principle can help you to avoid a lifetime of frustration.

The dream of "more" is a mental pacifier. It never solves a problem.

This is a book for realists.

Face up to your economic limitations whatever they may be. At the same time, begin *tomorrow morning* to enjoy a happier way of life. First step: *Find the way to become a better purchasing agent for yourself and your family.*

In this book: a three way plan

The purchasing agent for a large industry (or buyer for a large department store) considers three factors when he (or she) starts out to buy.

1. How shall I pay for this merchandise to get the most for my money?

2. What sources can I count on to give me the best buys?

3. What are my major needs, my secondary needs, my minor needs?

To help you buy as a good purchasing agent buys, this book is divided into three parts.

Part One analyzes your spending power.

You are richer than you know. What's more, you will become richer (even without a salary increase) as you put to work the simple principles explained here. Once you learn how to plug up hidden "leaks" in your present method of operation, and end expensive duplications in your long range planning, your financial picture will brighten. Other assets you do not even know you have will expand your buying ability. Your purchasing budget will double itself right before your eyes.

Part Two gives you a list of sources for whatever it is you want to purchase. You will learn when to buy what at local department stores, what items are always marked down as come-ons at discount stores, how to buy at an auction. Long before you have finished this section you will become truly sophisticated about the ways of the market place, whether you are buying at home or half way around the world. *You will be given specific information about how to bargain.*

Part Three tells you how to cut expenses at least 30% in your 10 major categories of spending. Here are three examples of the results you can expect:

> *Food:*   You can eat in a good restaurant or dine at home, whichever you prefer. But you will spend only 70% of what you are now spending.
>
> *Shelter:* Even though your mortgage or rent payments are fixed, you can still make that 30% slash.
>
> *Clothing*: You will spend less on your wardrobe, but you will be better dressed than ever before.

This book provides the key to living as you have always wanted to live, *without anxiety.* To attain this, your attitude toward money must change.

Money is nice to buy things with, that's all

Many years ago, when our eldest daughter, Susan, was a little girl seven years old, she asked one day "What would you ever do with money if you couldn't buy things with it?" She thought out her own answer. "I suppose you could spin it," she said, "or look at the pictures." She summed up her philosophy: "But if that's all you could do with money, nobody would want it much." Her good, young mind was telling her right then what Benjamin Franklin concluded a couple of hundred years before she was born. "Money is simply a medium of exchange," is what he said. Or as Susan put it, "Something to buy things with—that's all that money is."

Dollar bills are trading cards, that's all. Think of money as a medium of exchange and you will expect, and get, a good trade for every bill you put out.

Dollars and substitutes for dollars

The more trading cards you have, the more you can buy. Fortunately, dollar bills are just some of the trading cards available to you. In Part One of this book you will find you have trading cards that are far more valuable than dollars.

Your aim: good living

This is not a book for misers. Neither is it a manual for racketeers.

You will find no suggestions here for gypping the government on your income tax return, smuggling things through customs, or pulling the wool over a seller's eyes. No trickery, but follow suggestions here and you will live better for less money, and your life will be relaxed.

"We must have a fair degree of worldly goods," said Aristotle 3,000 years ago. "Poverty makes one stingy and grasping, while possessions give one that freedom from care and greed which is the source of aristocratic ease and charm."

This book points out marks of quality in clothes, furniture, architecture, art, *everything*. Learn them and you will automatically pass up shoddy merchandise and turn to superior craftsmanship and design.

Do you want a shortcut to security? You will find that here, but you will find more. Presented here for the first time is a revolutionary new system of selective spending. Learn this system and your life will be a life of plenty to the end of your days.

A few of the immediate results that will come from reading this book

1. Next week's meals will be more exciting, yet your food bills will go down.
2. You will begin to dress better, yet you will spend less money for clothes.
3. Your savings will increase if you want them to.
4. Your home will be a "conversation piece." So will the parties you give.
5. The work you do will become more meaningful. You will automatically become a better business man or woman.
6. Your next vacation will be the most glamorous trip of your life.
7. You will make a better deal on your house, your car, your boat—all the things you buy or sell.
8. The gifts you give will be more dramatic.
9. Your taste will improve.

Contents

13

Part One

Beefing up
your cash on hand

1

More Dollars
for What You Want

The way to get is to want.

Do you want a new car? A new Plymouth or a Ford or a Chevrolet?

Do you need more living space? Do you want to build an annex on your house or move into a larger apartment with one more bedroom?

How would you like a good long vacation? Want to cruise the Great Lakes or rent a cabin in the Rockies or listen to old time jazz down in New Orleans?

Dreams?

Not at all.

With wise planning, you can get whatever it is that you want. In fact by following suggestions in this book, you can get more than you have ever dared to want. Most people do not want enough.

Think again about that car.

If you could have what you *really* want, would you order instead of a medium priced car, a Chrysler or a Lincoln or a Buick?

You can have the car you want.

And about that extra living space? Are you settling for the annex because you think you can't afford a new house? Or, if you live in an apartment, are you sure that extra bedroom is all you want? Wouldn't you rather live in a duplex or a penthouse or buy a cooperative?

Say to yourself, "I can live wherever I want to live," and believe it, because this is a truth.

For your next vacation, would you like to cruise the Caribbean in your own boat? Or live for a whole year in Nepal? Or buy a permanent place in Hawaii where the whole family can go year after year?

There is a way to travel anywhere you want to go for far less than you now believe possible.

This book will point the way to getting whatever it is that you want. So as a starting point: *Don't be afraid to want. Your want is the goal that helps you achieve.*

The first big step

Getting what you want takes money. If you have little or no cash after your monthly bills are paid, extracting extra dollars from your present income may seem to be an impossibility. This is a fallacy. Finding added dollars is an easy matter once you revise your attitude toward your present income.

If you live on a salary or income that comes to you in checks once or twice a month, you undoubtedly think of your finances on a month-to-month basis. How much comes in? How much are you obligated to pay out? How much, if anything, is left over for what you want?

This way of thinking leads to discouragement. The average American has so many needs each month, he has little money left over to apply toward either big or little wants. As a result, his leftover money seems of such little account he spends it another way.

This is a dead end street. Follow it, and ten years from now you will be living a frustrated, pay-as-you-get life. Yet, even without making any more money, you can get off this economic treadmill.

Printed here for you to read and re-read, is the simple step that will show you the way to a sounder economic life: *Look at your finances as they might appear on an annual statement, not as they look from month to month.*

Right now, put down on a sheet of paper what you expect to earn in the next 12 months beginning with the first of next month. On this same sheet, take a few minutes to estimate your basic annual expenses. (If you know what you spend for food each month, for rent or mortgage payments, for utilities, for insurance, etc., multiply each of these figures by 12. Put down your estimated income tax for next year and any special costs, like college.) Subtract your anticipated expenses from your anticipated income. The remaining figure is what you should be able to count on to spend as you want to spend in the 12 months to come.

Figure your income and outgo on an *annual* rather than a monthly basis, and you benefit in two specific ways. (1) You automatically cut down on the high cost of credit; and (2) you get better buys by paying cash.

Facing up to the high cost of credit

As long as you live on a month-to-month basis you are a sucker for "only so much a month" advertising. You reason, for instance, that you can easily pay the small monthly installments necessary to buy the color TV which is advertised at the bargain price of $399. Nothing to it!

But think of your income on an annual basis, and you will react differently. Do you want to allocate $204 next year for a TV set? (That's what your payments will amount to.) And if so, can't you start with that $204 in cash and get a better buy on your TV? Look at your monthly payment agreement and you will see that even after agreeing to spend that first $204, you may still have *two more years* to go!

Once you lick the month-to-month payment habit, you will see that *credit comes high.* It is safe to figure that anything bought on a three-year installment loan will cost at least 25% more than what you pay in cash.

Suppose you are buying your house for $25,000? You can get a mortgage from the bank amounting to 80% of the sale price. So you pay $5,000 down on the house and agree to pay the bank $20,000 at 6% over a period of 25 years.

You will pay for your $20,000 advance a total of $38,661.00 *Or $18,661.00 in interest.*

As a good business person, you can find nothing objectionable about a banker's need to make money. Nor do we. Our only point is that it is a good idea to be aware of what the money you are borrowing for a house or anything else is costing you. You can't cut the high cost of credit unless you look at this cost.

Shopping for money

Recently, a young couple told us about buying a house originally priced at $16,900 for only $16,000. As we talked, we learned the interest rate on their $14,000 mortgage was 1% higher than it would have been had they worked out a plan available to them at a nearby bank. Spread over a 25 year period, this 1% makes for an extra payment of $8.35 a month or $2505 in all. $2505! If they had shopped for money as carefully as they shopped for the house, they could have furnished their house and handsomely. Shop for money as carefully as you shop for anything else. Be sure you know the true interest rate you pay for *everything!* A mortgage agreement is relatively easy to understand, but other contracts are more complicated. When you start to sign the innocent looking contract for a $1795 used car, you may have a change of heart when you discover that the easy monthly payments conceal a 20% interest charge plus hidden insurance, plus a lump sum payment to come after regular installments are finished. In reality, you may be paying $2875 for that car. Is it worth it?

The time to avoid a poor contract is before you sign it. So be careful.

Interest rates may be confusing to you. In our present merchandising climate, when charges are deliberately buried for sales-making reasons, only a good accountant can be expected to understand all the ramifications that appear in contracts. If you agree to purchase anything on credit (or borrow money for the purchase of anything), be aware that you are going to pay dearly for this purchase. Before signing a sizeable contract, pay $10 to an accountant to look it over.[1] He will determine the true cost of whatever it is you are buying by adding in all costs, hidden and otherwise. You may be shocked out of buying.

Existing contracts

If you have been buying on the installment plan as a way of life, take your current contracts to an accountant, too. Much to your surprise you may find that in order to end some contracts before the agreed upon time, you may be forced to pay a "pay off" premium. Never again sign a contract of this kind.

Certainly, a good clear look at the interest charges that accompany most time-buying agreements will encourage you to buy on time only when this method is absolutely necessary, and then to buy carefully. At all other times, you will want to pay as you go.

Cash buys more than credit

For the dramatic bargains which you will come upon at auctions, second hand stores, and in out-of-the-way shops and galleries, you need cash. So resent everything that depletes your cash on hand without giving excellent value in return.

Even when you are not buying unusual merchandise, you pay less when you buy from a cash-and-carry store than you do from a store that provides special services including a charge account. The cost of special services is reflected in a mark-up of merchandise.

When you charge mechandise, just as when you buy on the installment plan, you are paying for the use of another person's money. (The merchant has already put out money to get the

---

[1] For a good customer, an accountant will perform this service for nothing.

merchandise into your hands. You are paying him for the use of his money.) We have already seen that money comes high. By paying for merchandise alone and refusing to pay for credit, you can increase the buying power of every dollar you take to the market place.

More dollars per year

Look at your finances in terms of annual, rather than monthly, income and outgo, and you will find almost immediately that you have more dollars to spend.

2

All Your Bookkeeping
on One Sheet of Paper

Budgeting your every penny allows for no fun in spending, no spur-of-the-moment buying, no generosity on gift occasions. Budgeting, we think, is a dreary business. We do not recommend it.

Bookkeeping, on the other hand, gives you an accurate picture of how your money goes. It provides a record that saves you time and money when you make out your income tax. It is important for advance planning. The only trouble is that the average bookkeeping system takes time and skill.

For your convenience, we have worked out a system easy enough for a child to manage. Yet it is efficient, because it allows you to see at a glance what you will take in this year, what you will pay out for regular expenses, what you will have left for special purchases.

You keep no books with this system. All you need is one sheet of paper.

One glance tells all

On a blank sheet of paper make four vertical lines, sectioning off the paper into three columns. At the top of the first column write Gross Income. At the top of the second column write Gross Expenses. At the top of the third column, write New Purchases.

Your paper will look like this.

Gross Income	Gross Expenses	New Purchases

This one sheet of paper is the only set of books you will keep during the coming year.

In the first left hand column put down your anticipated income for the next 12 months. (If your total income tax is withheld, consider your take-home pay as your total income. If you pay your own income tax, put down your total income. Later, put your anticipated income tax in the second column.)

In the coming year, the figure at the top of the left hand column may change. You may lose your job, or you may not succeed in a business venture as you now believe you will. In either of these cases, your income will be less. On the other hand, you may get a raise or make more money from some other source or come into an unexpected inheritance. In this case, you will add the sum of the windfall to the figure now in this column.

In the second or middle column, write down all of your regular expenses. Rent (or mortgage payments), food, gas and electricity, heat, transportation, normal repairs, normal clothing expenses. Anticipate your year's outgo for each, penciling in each figure in parentheses below each major classification. Add the figures in this column. The total again is only a working figure. Before the year is out, it may change. Your rent may go up; you may be transferred to a new location where rent is higher; the cost of your transportation may go up.

More than likely, however, the total for this column will be much less than you now anticipate by the end of this year. Certainly, that will be your aim, because the less you spend for habitual expenses, the more you will have for new purchases and investments. Later in the book, you will find specific ways to cut your routine expenses to 70% of what you are now paying, or more.

But for a starting point, figure these expenses as you are currently operating. The sum of the figure in this middle column represents your gross annual expenses.

Now, subtract the sum of the figures in the middle column from your gross income in the first column. This is what you will have to spend for special purchases. Write this figure at the top of the third column. Underneath put down the major purchases you know you will be making. Write down overcoat, if you plan to buy one; vacation trip to Florida (or anywhere else); summer camp for children; a new roof for the house. Write in pencil, putting in parentheses after each item what you now expect to pay.

Does your budget allow for all the purchases you want to make? *Probably not.* If not, you have four choices.

1. Do without
2. Expand your gross income
3. Cut your expenses as listed in column two
4. Buy everything in column three for less than you now believe possible

We do not advocate in this book *doing without* unless your wants are much too great for your income. You must be the judge of that. So we will not talk to the first point. Nor will we address ourselves to the second point. Expanding your gross income is a good idea, but it is not the subject of this book. We will confine ourselves to items three and four. In this book you will find suggestions for cutting your current everyday expenses. And on page after page you will find ways to buy new things for from 20 to 90% less than the going price.

Advantages inherent in this system

By estimating what your purchasing fund will be for the year ahead, you can buy as a professional buys. Certain advantages will be immediately forthcoming. (1) You will plan your buying to avoid the peak buying periods, when merchandise is high priced. (Example: You will not buy lawn furniture in the early summer, fishing equipment at vacation time, snow suits in November.) (2) Knowing what you are going to be buying a year in advance will give you time to shop around. (3) Bargaining will be easier because you will not be buying out of need.

When you absolutely have to buy, don't

Think back to the last time you overpaid for something, whether that something was a room in a strange hotel, a hat for a church function (or a funeral) or an automobile repair job.

Chances are that you paid more than you wanted to pay because you bought without premeditation. There are once-in-a-lifetime times when this kind of buying can't be helped. If you and two children are freezing in a stalled car in a snowbank, you can't take time to haggle with the first man with a tow truck who says he will pull you out for a price. But there are few emergency situations which are this critical. The average emergency is self-imposed.

Let us take, for example, the suburban woman who has been meaning to have her best dinner dress shortened, but just hasn't got around to it. Her husband calls from the city one morning telling her to come in that night for dinner with friends from out of town. Immediately she has to have that dinner dress shortened. Right this day! She manages this, but not without over-paying the tailor, the baby-sitter and the cab driver. The cost for her dinner in the city is monumental.

But looking back at that day at the end of the year, will she say that the need to get that one particular dress shortened was really a necessity? Was there no alternative?

The next time you find yourself hurrying to buy something because you have to buy it today, hold still for one thought. "What else can I do?" is the thing to ask yourself. "What is there to do if I don't buy?" Out of this kind of thinking an alternative will come which may be a better solution to your immediate problem than the one you are now considering. And, certainly, it should cost you less money. Hurry-up buying is expensive. "Necessity never made a bargain," is the way Ben Franklin put it.

If you are out to save money at the market place, do not buy out of need. Make do for the time being with a substitute. Then, do your buying. You will come out far ahead, and you might like the substitute better!

Advance planning saves money

Planning for purchases before the actual need arises will save you money. What's more, your one-page bookkeeping system will bring order into your life. Tape your account sheet on the wall of your study or kitchen or bedroom. Refer to it often, penciling in changes, price cuts, coming needs. By looking squarely at your coming needs you will be able to meet them long before they become urgent.

The buys you get as a result of this system will be almost un-believable—*even to you!*

3

Nine Other Trading Cards to Use Along with Dollars

Dollars are powerful trading cards. But you have other cards to trade. So do not be discouraged if your income does not seem to be large enough to cover all your wants. Also, do not become panicky if you find yourself so involved in installment buying that you have little cash left over for new purchases.

Just face facts. This next year may be the time to cut back on all cash spending to pay off your present installment contracts.

Cut back to the sleeping point

Bernard Baruch, one of the world's greatest natural economists, had a course that he followed when he found himself staying awake nights fretting about his stock market holdings.

"In my younger days," he said, "I heard someone, I forget who, remark 'Sell to the sleeping point.' That is a gem of wisdom of the purest ray serene. When we are worried, it is because our subconscious mind is trying to telegraph us some message of warning. The wisest course is to sell to the point where one stops worrying."

If you are worrying about money, use all of your available cash to pay off your obligations. In doing this, you will not necessarily deprive yourself.

The fine art of trading without money

We all have trading cards more precious than gold.

A good trader knows what cards he holds instinctively. But knowing how to exchange something other than a dollar (or along with a dollar) in the marketplace is an art. You may have to learn this art. Learn it well, and you will never feel a lack.

One glance at the following list should open your eyes to tradeable assets you possess which you may now be overlooking.

Nine priceless trading cards

1. THINGS

Think of the things which you no longer use which are in your attic or basement or closets or on your land? Do you have skis you don't use? An old wedding dress? Ice cream chairs from a long forgotten business? Wood on your land? All are important to someone. Make a written list of everything you own which you are willing to give up in exchange for one of the new things on your list which you want to buy next year.

2. TALENT

What do you do easily that all your friends find difficult? Write a good letter? Play the piano? Build things? List these talents under the things you have to trade. You can trade your talents.

3. INFLUENCE

List the clubs you belong to. Are there many members in each? Do you have many uncles, aunts, and cousins in the community? Do people follow what you do automatically? Do you write a column or put on a radio show? If so, your every word is worth money. Put these activities on your list.

4. TIME

How many hours a day can you donate to a project, even though you can't leave home? Your left-over time is invaluable to someone. Make a note of the hours of time you have in a day that you can trade to someone for something you want.

5. SERVICE

Can you drive a car? Type? Lay a flagstone terrace? Transplant a tree? Keep children in line? Anything else? Others are willing to pay for such services, or better yet, to trade something of importance to you for such services. List what you *can do.*

6. SPACE (AND EQUIPMENT)

Do you have an empty attic, basement, garage? Space is something you can trade. Or do you have a bulldozer, a mower, even a wheelbarrow? Somebody has need for all of these things.

7. KNOWLEDGE

Do you know local history better than anyone around? A writer can use you. Know French cooking? A professional test kitchen or bakery or delicatessen may give you food products in exchange for getting information from you. Know ballet but don't dance anymore? An artist may find your knowledge invaluable. Every piece of knowledge you have can be traded for something.

8. COMMON SENSE

Can you figure things out? Unravel problems that seem knotty to others? Simplify life? Does everybody around you consult you about things that don't seem at all involved to you? Your gift is rare. It can be traded.

9. GRATITUDE

Strangely enough, the ability to say "thank you" (and mean it) brings good things to you faster than any other quality. People will do things for you for nothing.

As a beginning exercise in trading, let yourself dream for a moment of something you would like to buy that costs less than $50 but still constitutes an extravagance in your life.

Keep this want in mind as you read through the possible trades that are open to you.

1. Trade something you no longer need

Suppose you want a round wormy chestnut table for your living room. (This year wormy chestnut, because of its rarity, is "in." In New York, a wrought iron table with a marble top is priced at $39.95; the same table with a wormy chestnut top is priced at $49.95.)

If you live in a state where chestnut was used extensively before the blight in the early 1900s, you may be able to find a slab of chestnut which you can have cut for your table top.

Let's say that you see, in your neighborhood, a hen house (no longer used) which is made of chestnut. (We found just such a dilapidated hen house on the farm we bought in Connecticut.) What can you offer the farmer that he will find of more value to him than the door? Six or eight of your laying hens, if you also are a farmer. Two pretty dresses your daughter has outgrown, if you have a daughter and know he has a daughter. An electric blanket which you got for Christmas but never use because you already have two.

The trick in trading with the farmer (or anyone) is to know (1) how to approach him and (2) what you have to offer that will please him as much as what you want will please you. The best approach is the simple approach. Simply tell the farmer, in this case, that you have been looking for a chestnut door, and see that he has one. Tell him that you have something to trade that you think will make sense to him. He may not accept the trade you have to offer, but certainly his curiosity will make him listen to your offer. Once having gained his attention, you can go on from there.

Let's say that he accepts the electric blanket and gives you the door. Your next step is to take the door to your local carpentry shop and have two round 30-inch table tops cut from the slab of chestnut. You now have two table tops. It will be a simple thing now for you to trade a beautiful wormy chestnut table top to a furniture designer, decorator, or antique dealer for a wrought iron stand.

End result: You have a handsome $49.95 coffee table in exchange for a $16.75 electric blanket which you got as a gift (plus the few dollars outlay to the carpenter).

Here's a trade any college girl can make. Say she wants a new dress for a prom at a nearby school. She can suggest a trade to her roommate. "I'll trade you that coral colored cashmere sweater of mine and my hockey stick for that black Estevez cocktail dress you don't wear any more." If her roommate likes the sweater and is signed up for hockey next semester and has had her wear of the Estevez dress, our college girl has a deal.

The trick in trading is to come up with a suggestion that ties in with another person's needs.

Do you have an old banged up typewriter? Trade it to the boy next door for a croquet set. Do you want an enormous new lamp for the living room? Think of someone who is moving from a large place to a small one, and offer to trade that person a space-saving item (a coffee table that doubles as a dining table, for instance). Or go to a wallpaper shop and ask the owner if he can get you a wallpaper printing roller that you can have wired for a lamp. Trade him a filing cabinet or a roll top desk or a collection of old wallpaper books. The principle of trading things can be as easy for you today as it was when you were trading marbles in the school yard long ago.

When trading things for things, here are six points to keep in mind:

- Collect things and/or save things, not because you may need them but because someone else may need them. Things that you don't trade at the end of the year you can give away as gifts.
- When you want something, think of someone who has what you want.
- Do some thinking about this person. Has he outgrown his need for whatever it is you want? What are his current interests? Do some research. Then talk.
- Don't try to work out a dollar-for-dollar deal.

- Do suggest a trade that makes sense to the other person. Offer something that the other person really wants in exchange for something he will hardly miss.
- Do not insist that everything you acquire be brand new.

Many persons overlook the possibility of trading things, just as they overlook this second trading card:

2. *Trade your talent*

Here is the best definition of talent we can find. *"Doing easily what others find difficult, is talent."*

What can you do easily that your friends and acquaintances find hard to do? Are you good at public speaking? Do you have a sense of rhythm, the best dancer in the crowd? Are you game-minded, win more prizes (or money) when playing bridge or gin rummy or Canasta? Can you sing well? Cook better than most? Are you better at sports—golf, bowling, tennis? Can you draw or paint? Do you have a feeling for design? Do you have a flair for decorating? Are you a good organizer? Are you good at carpentry? Horseback riding? Do you have a green thumb?

You can trade your *have* to *have nots,* and they will appreciate this more than money.

Here are some examples of the way talent can be traded:

(1) A book editor near us wanted sauna treatments in New York. "I will do a brochure for you," he told the health service, "in exchange for $475 worth of massage and sauna treatments." He made the deal. He did three suggestions for a brochure, one was accepted. Then he did all copy and photography. The brochure is now given to customers. He has sauna treatments at no cost.

(2) Two years ago, Ernie Henfeld, an artist friend of ours who then worked for a commercial art studio, decided that his real talent lay in painting portraits. He came to us with a suggestion.

"I will do one of your portraits (Mrs. Kinney's probably)

for nothing," he said, "if you will let me use your garden two mornings a week to work on portraits of other people."

We accepted quickly. And we now have a good portrait hanging in our stairwell.

Now what did Ernie Henfeld gain from the arrangement?

- He had a pleasant garden studio in the heart of New York in which to work two mornings a week.
- He had a finished portrait to show to prospective clients.
- His work hangs in our home where many people come and go, and calls attention every day to his talent, which is big.
- The portrait became one of a group of five portraits by the end of the summer, the necessary number to prove to an agent that this man was worth handling on a percentage basis.
- Doing the portrait led to publicity for Ernie. (Example, this page in this book.)

By now, Ernie Henfeld's work is being recognized by New York celebrities, his portraits hang in elegant homes, his work is displayed in well known restaurants. He now has his own studio on 58th Street. Putting his God-given talent to work opened up a whole new world.

(3) I. B. Hale, an executive at General Dynamics at Fort Worth, Texas, and captain of the Texas Christian football team in '38, is an expert bridge player. During his three weeks' vacation from General Dynamics each year, Mr. Hale and his wife, also an expert, go on a cruise (this year to the Mediterranean) with all expenses paid in exchange for overseeing the duplicate tournament on board ship.

"If a man has talent and cannot use it," said Thomas Wolfe, "he has failed. If he has a talent and uses only half of it, he has partly failed. If he has a talent and learns somehow to use the whole of it, he has gloriously succeeded and won a satisfaction and a triumph few men ever know."

Begin to put your talent to work, whatever it may be. You may find as you do that you are a pace-setter, as well as talented. Then, you have the power to influence others.

3. *Trade your power to influence others*

Fifty years ago Gabrielle (the legendary Coco) Chanel, then the owner of a small boutique in Deauville, went to the race track, became chilly, and borrowed a sweater from a jockey. In a week, all of fashionable Deauville was in sweaters. Even then, the woman who was to launch Chanel No. 5 (which now grosses nine million dollars a year and outsells all other perfumes in 140 countries) and create the classic Chanel suit ($800 a suit at her House of Chanel and the most copied suit in Paris) was a born pace-setter.

One day Coco wore sailor pants in Venice so that she could step in and out of gondolas gracefully. Soon, not only European women, but also Americans, began wearing pants. Coming up from Cannes one winter with a tan, she made other women look washed-out. Suddenly, the sun-tan look was in.

If you have this pace-setting quality, capitalize on it. It is worth all kinds of money.

QUESTIONS TO ASK YOURSELF

1. If you (or your wife) were first in your circle to send out personal letters on stationery with florid, monogrammed lettering described by Tiffany's as lettering "like the engraving on your grandfather's watch" would most of your friends follow suit?

2. When one of your children join a subteen-age dancing group, do all the children of your friends want to join?

3. If you sign up to go on a charter trip to Europe, will many of your friends decide to go along?

4. Do acquaintances try to make you beholden to them—do they pick up your check, invite you to their homes before you quite get around to invite them, do unsolicited favors for you?

5. Do you consider yourself lucky?

If you have five "yes" answers, you have that unique something that makes others want to do what you do.

You may wonder what that last question about luck has to do with your leadership qualities. It tells a great deal.

Visiting Victor Keppler of the Famous Photographers School in Westport, Conn., we came to know much about the ten men on his Guiding Faculty. They are tops in their field. Look at the list: Richard Avedon, Richard Beattie, Joseph Costa, Arthur d'Arazien, Alfred Eisenstaedt, Harry Garfield, Philippe Halsman, Irving Penn, Bert Stern, Ezra Stoller.

Not long ago each of these men was asked "Do you consider yourself lucky?" And each said quickly, "Yes." Yet, when asked to explain, each said in one of a variety of ways that he *really* believed *luck is either built into the character of an individual or it isn't*. As Philippe Halsman put it, "A photographer who is lucky has the ability to anticipate that something is going to happen and be ready for it. At a bullfight, he captures the crucial moment. The unlucky photographer, on the other hand, does not have this ability to anticipate and be ready for what is going to happen. He is changing his film when the bull is killed."

If you have the ability to anticipate when something is going to happen or is going to "catch on" whether it is a fashion, a vacation spot, or a political philosophy, you can use this talent as coin.

Such talent is rare, so don't despair if you do not possess this. You have other cards to trade.

4. Trade your leftover time

If you are under 25 years old and you have minutes of your day when you don't have anything to do, think of the person you know who most loves his or her work. Perhaps it's a busy contractor who may have six jobs going. He runs here, there, everywhere keeping his men busy, his customers happy, and the houses he has contracted for going up. Or it may be a successful artist who resents every minute he has to spend away from his canvas. Or it may be a great salesman (of vacuum cleaners, or advertising space, or automobiles or real estate) who loves to sell and really hates doing anything else much.

Here's where you can make a trade.

Let's take the artist, for instance.

Are his paintings really great? Would you like to own one?

Go to the artist and tell him or her that you have *time*. (Maybe you go to school and you have three hours a day you can give to his problems.) Tell the artist that there must be many things in his life that he feels that he is neglecting. Maybe he has a little boy whom he should be reading to. Perhaps he has started a rose garden that is dying from lack of care. Maybe he needs someone to help him straighten up his studio. Tell this man that you will give him three hours a day for several weeks in exchange for a painting.

Then do his leftover chores. If the artist does not appeal to you, go to a teacher or a doctor. We all know about the boy in a small town who drove with the family doctor on his rounds so the doctor could sleep between calls. He, in turn, became a dedicated doctor.

The trick is, in the beginning, to offer to do *anything*. Offer to do all odd jobs that come up in the life of a writer or salesman or doctor too busy to get them done.

It is more practical to trade time with someone of your own sex than with someone of the opposite sex. As a girl, you know how to insist on the right blue rinse at the beauty shop for the woman teacher you have decided to help. If you're a boy, you know how to stain new floorboards to look like old ones to help the contractor you've decided to trade your time to.

If you offer to trade time for something other than money, you will get a ready audience. Obviously a painter can give you a painting. But what can the contractor give you? He can give you the boards and plans for a cabin you can build in the woods. The teacher can give you lessons in whatever you want to learn, because the dedicated teacher can teach *anything*.

"How," you may be asking, "can the person with no time to

make beauty shop appointments and to fill the car with gas and to buy clothes as they wear out have time to design a cabin in the woods or give lessons to me?"

The answer lies in the other person's love of work.

We have talked here of the dedicated workman who has no time, and we have talked also of the young man or woman with time that he or she doesn't know what to do with. Why haven't we talked of the older man or woman with time on his hands? Can't he or she make a trade?

The older man or woman surely has some special work he likes to do that is considered important by many. It may not bring in much money in the marketplace, but this is work he or she likes to do. If you have work you prefer to all others, be proud of this work, whether it is mending, cake baking, chair caning, or hedge clipping. Trade the work you like to do, once you find it, and not your time.

5. *Trade your services*

"He profits most who serves best."

That is the motto for Rotary International. No truer words have ever been put down on paper. If you perfect a skill which serves the purpose of another, you will not want. Let me give you an example.

We live in Connecticut, but we keep an apartment in New York. We drive the 80 miles to New York at least once a week, but seldom can we accommodate regular travelers because we go in at odd hours.

Last week we had a call. A woman told us that she had heard us as we were being interviewed on a radio program about this book. She had been a professional "shopper" for stores, checking up on the sales ability of their clerks. She called to offer us a trade. "I have to go into New York at least once a week," she told us, "when I have special 'shopping' assignments. Naturally, I am always grateful to get a ride in." As we listened she spelled out her proposition. "You said on the radio," she said, "that you drive to New York several times a month. Now, if you would let me ride in and out with you, I could 'shop' for you in some of the stores you will be writing about. I could give you my findings as we ride home."

Through this arrangement we have learned of many little bargain shops; where merchants plant their come-on merchandise and why; how fast merchandise is marked down when it is apparent that it will not sell; what days are the Big Sale days. From us, our "shopper" gets a ride down and back whenever she wants to go, and she stays in our apartment if she happens to be caught in New York for later than we can stay in. We both benefit, *and no money is exchanged.*

We once got a boat, a $5,000 mahogany inboard (original price), on a trade, and paid exactly nothing. The owner of a small advertising agency inherited it, and offered it to us for $800. We said "$700, but we would like to trade for it by doing advertising copy and layouts." We advanced $700; he paid us not $700, but $1800 by assigning us work at our regular per diem rate. The boat we think of as free.

Perfect a skill or service and learn how to trade it, and you can write your own ticket.

Out in LaCrosse, Wisconsin, a caterer works from her own home and makes fabulous coconut cakes. She provides her chiropodist with a cake a month, come rain or shine. In exchange she has her feet cared for whenever she needs this kind of attention. She never pays a cent for pedicures—and he gets his coconut cake, which he happens to love.

SERVICES THAT ARE APPRECIATED

If you can write, you can do publicity for a restaurant for a dinner a week; for a resort hotel in exchange for an annual vacation there; for a bridge club in exchange for lessons; for a dancing class in exchange for dancing lessons for your child, etc., etc. Publicity is one of the greatest trade-in services in the world. An artist can do signs for windows, brochures, architectural drawings. But there are other skills just as appreciated. If you are a good bookkeeper, keep books for any of the above businesses in exchange for the same rewards. Ditto for anyone who can take good photographs, do good window displays, do novel flower arrangements. The same goes for an accountant who can help with income tax returns.

Decide what you want—to eat in a fine restaurant once a week, have a permanent pass to the local theaters or motion pictures, free tickets to local entertainments, take bridge, dancing, or music lessons, get a piano or car or house at a discount? Now what service can *you* offer that the other person has a need for? That's the answer you must search for. Once you find it, your trading card is a wild card. You can play it on anything!

You should be beginning to understand now how trades can be made without cash. And there are more examples to come. For instance, you can trade space.

6. *Trade extra space*

Even six inches of space (if the space happens to be in a store window) makes for a valuable trading card. Give the motion picture manager space to put up a small billboard, and he will give you a weekly pass to the movies.

All trades that involve the giving away of space are not this direct, but all space is appreciated.

Do you have space to store a boat? Trade it for hours of free boating next summer.

Do you have a great big dry attic where you can store costumes for the local summer stock company? You should have a season ticket in exchange for offering this. Or maybe a traveling hardware salesman can leave summer merchandise there that he doesn't want to carry day-to-day along the road. Here's your chance to get your next year's garden tools. Or maybe a small local dress shop would like to store merchandise there not yet ready for the floor. Let them. In exchange you may be able to get your clothes wholesale.

A big barn on your property can save a man money. Make a

trade with that man. Let him use your barn for storage in exchange for giving you a car at a discount, if he's a garage owner; lawn furniture at a discount if he's a furniture store owner; milk for breakfast if he is a farmer and wants to store his hay in there.

The most valuable space is living space. Do you have a room in your home or space that can be converted into a small utility apartment? A working mother with a small child may become your cook in exchange for this. (The working mother can work during the day, leaving her child in a nursery. Then, she can pick up her child, come home to the utility apartment and get your dinner in exchange for her living.) This is a good thing for you if you can afford the space and you need a cook.

Space can be as small as a chair, and still be worth a pocketful of gold, if that space is a theater seat at a hit show or an envied chair at the captain's table on a ship. Promise someone space for living, storage, display or just sitting, and you have a trading card that can always be played.

7. *Trade from your store of knowledge*

The expert in any field commands respect. But sometimes to trade knowledge takes some doing. However, there is usually someone who has need for the information you possess.

Many retired businessmen serve as consultants to younger persons in the same field. These consultants are paid an annual fee for giving information that can help a company make money or recruit men or make a better product. If you have knowledge in one area (as the retired business man knows his former business) your temptation will be to discount its importance. The information you have stored up during the years, you think to yourself, is something anyone could find out if they just looked around. This is true, but busy men and women don't have time to research the field you have lived in so closely and for so long. To get from you in a few minutes what it might take them months or years to find out is worth money, or a very handsome substitute.

Were you born outside of the United States? The knowledge

you have stored up can be of extreme value to a writer who wants accurate background material for a play or a story; to a merchant who wants to import or to export merchandise; to an advertiser who wants to know what your people respond to; to politicians who want to appeal to an ethnic group; to travel bureaus, to artists, to museum collectors. If you speak the language of that country, you already know how this skill can be put to use. You must have been asked to translate letters or manuscripts, serve as an interpreter for someone visiting from your former country, or give lessons to someone going there.

When trading knowledge, look for someone who has a need for information you possess. Then suggest your trade. Perhaps a TV or motion picture producer may be doing a story about your birthplace. He may take you with him if your knowledge of the country is deep and you are sensitive to undercurrents.

Having grown up in a lumber camp you may know everything there is to know about wood and how it reacts and interacts with chemicals. Your knowledge will be invaluable to a man starting a small mill. Trade your knowledge for logs to build a lodge. (This means, of course, that you do not want a job in the mill. The knowledge we are talking about now is knowledge that you can use as a trading card, something to use *outside* of your livelihood.)

Did your father run a meat market? The restaurant owner down the street who is a better promoter than he is a cook, can save money with what you know. Buy his meats for him and help his chef plan his menus. In exchange, of course, you eat free.

You may have grown up on Cape Cod. When friends go there to visit, they ask you where to stay, what to see, where to eat. You give them the information. In exchange they bring you a miniature Sandwich glass cup for your collection. This is an *unspoken* trade.

Now we are urging you to speak out with your trade. (In the Cape trade, you will not make a spoken trade because the need of the travelers is purely personal, not commercial.) But begin translating what you do in personal trading to commercial trading.

You will be surprised at the value that is put on the knowledge which you are now taking for granted.

One day a man working for a small house organ for one of the big oil companies came to us and asked us how to break into advertising. "Go to the agency," we told him, "that handles the advertising for the oil company you have been writing about. And ask for a writer's job at $9,000 a year." (This was twice what he was getting as editor.) Much to his surprise, but not to ours, he got the job on the first interview. The agency needs his deep-down knowledge to do a better advertising job.

Once you pin-point what knowledge you have, look around for people who have a commercial need for this. You can make a deal easily.

8. *Trade your common sense*

"Nothing astonishes men so much as common sense and plain dealing." Emerson said that, and there is just as much truth in this today as there was at the time of the Industrial Revolution. Common sense in a business office is as refreshing as a cool drink of water. Often, it is more welcome than money. Do you have natural common sense? This test will tell you.

Check 1, 2 or 3 in each multiple choice answer at the end of each question below:

I.   There's a lot of truth to the saying "It's easy to get money from a bank if you don't need the money." (1) Yes (2) No (3) This is a silly statement.

II.   All professional packers for moving van companies are reluctant to pack (1) jewelry valued at over $10,000 (2) living plants (3) paintings not insured for full value.

III.   You will sell 10 times as much wax spray for furniture if you present it in one of these ways rather than in the others. Do you know which is the best way to present your product to women? (1) This is the best wax there is in an aerosol can. (2) This is a protective wax for fine furniture. (3) This is a wax that belongs on your dust cloth when you dust.

IV. If 38% of the people who watch a television commercial remember what the commercial said when they are called the next day, the commercial is (1) doing a little better than average job (2) doing a sensational job for the advertiser (3) doing a poor job.

V. When a banker decides how large a mortgage to give you on the house, he gives his first consideration to (1) your financial statement (2) the appraisal of the house (3) the real estate broker's appraisal of you and your worth.

VI. When you borrow $16,000 at 6% to buy a house on a 25 year mortgage, you will pay the mortgagor in 25 years (1) $27,500 (2) $19,682 (3) $30,927.

VII. When driving at a normal rate of speed on the highway it is wise to keep a car length behind the car in front of you because (1) you want to be able to stop without hitting the car in front if he should stop suddenly (2) you must leave room for the car behind you to pass if he wants to (3) you cannot see the signals of the driver up ahead if you are right on top of his car.

VIII. If you are in a store and decide to treat two children in your friend's car outside to ice cream cones, you will make them happiest by (1) taking each a different flavored cone as a surprise (2) surprising them with two identical cones with a familiar, but not too familiar flavor, like strawberry (3) going out first to select their orders.

IX. If a real estate agent comes to see your house which you are desperate to sell, will he be most excited about selling it if you (1) let him use his own judgment about how to sell it and for what price (2) provide him with a written fact sheet that gives him all vital statistics (3) help him to see how you have used the house and/or made money from renting the house so that he can pass that information on to prospects.

X. Food experts recommend that you buy ⅛ to ½ pound of boneless roast for each person you plan to serve. How much do you believe they recommend buying per person when you are serving pork back ribs? (1) ¾ to 1 pound (2) 1¼ to 2 pounds (3) ⅛ to ½ pound.

XI. Some campers spending a week in the woods have a very young dog along with them. They run into a hornets' nest and all are stung. In the excitement would you expect the stung dog to (1) run to its master and stay close beside him (2) run back to the tent and hide there (3) head out for home wherever that might be?

XII. If you are renting a home or apartment now, and think perhaps you should buy, here is a rule of thumb that will help you to know how much you can spend. Multiply what you are now spending for rent by 100. This will tell you the size of mortgage you can carry. (If you are paying $100 a month rent you can carry a $10,000 mortgage.) Add what you would have to pay for a down payment on a home with a $10,000 mortgage. That is at least $2,500. Add the down payment to the mortgage you can carry and you arrive at a sum of $12,500. That, according to this way of figuring, is the price of the home you can afford to buy. If you accept this theory but hold back from the thought of buying, you find yourself hesitating because (1) you know there will be unknown expenses not computed in this way of figuring and this makes you fearful (2) you know you will lose money if the price of your property should go down (3) you can live better by renting than you could if you lived in a house that this theory tells you you can afford.

The "common sense" person will answer each of these questions with the answer printed in this upside-down column.

8 IIX		8 IΛ
2 IX		2 Λ
1 X		1 ΛI
8 XI		8 III
2 IIIΛ		2 II
1 IIΛ		1 I

When someone has a problem you do not have to spell out this problem, just present the solution.

Say you are a dancing teacher. You need a ballroom one night a week to give lessons to young people. You know the hotel you want, but you can't afford the rent. You also know that the owner of the hotel has a daughter who is overly fat. Here is a case where you *don't* have to start your conversation with "Now you have a daughter who is fat and is undoubtedly a worry to you because of this." He knows she's fat and this does worry him. Offer to give dancing lessons to his daughter in exchange for the ballroom. He will see how dancing lessons can help his child.

Look at what the other fellow needs or what problem he is trying to solve. Then, arrange your barter.

9. The most welcome trade of all: gratitude

When you come to the end of this paragraph, close your eyes and think of the last person who has given time and thought to your needs. The person you are thinking of may not have done you a big favor, just a thoughtful one like bringing an unexpected cup of coffee to your desk in sympathy for your fatigue; calling you on an anniversary that others have forgotten; performing an unexpected courtesy in a group where you were suffering embarrassment. Think of the sensitivity that person had to have to your needs to be able to act as he or she acted, and you will begin to sense the true meaning of gratitude. *Close your eyes for 30 seconds and think with appreciation of a favor granted to you.* The person who feels real gratitude daily for any favor or courtesy or thoughtfulness expressed by another human being feels at all times the appreciation you have felt now with your eyes closed.

As you work to *feel* gratitude for favors done for you, you may feel phony. There are two ways to avoid this.

1. Don't *be* phony. Don't pretend to feel gratitude you don't feel. Save this deep-down appreciation we have been talking about for the times when you really are appreciative.

2. Don't express gratitude in advance in order to make something happen. When you manipulate a favor through pretended appreciation for what is coming, you waste the power that is within you.

Now, close your eyes and think of a person you have recently gone out of your way to do something nice for. Was your thoughtfulness received with gratitude?

Close your eyes and remember how some thoughtfulness you have expressed was received. Stay completely silent for 30 seconds.

If the person you have been thinking about was ungrateful, you now feel angry or sad. But if the person you went out of your way to please was truly grateful, you feel rewarded now. You are smiling.

This is all we have been wanting you to see. If you approach each day with gratitude for the good things that happened yesterday, more good things will happen today.

You cannot spend this trading card as you do the others. But feel gratitude and favors will come unbidden.

Closing thought: What about that $50 purchase you wanted to make when you started this chapter. Do you know how to get it now through a trade? Perhaps you will when you count your assets next.

COUNT YOUR ASSETS

Personal Trading Cards	*Grade Yourself from 1 to 10 (1 for a low number of assets in each category, 10 for a high number)*
THINGS	_____
TALENT	_____
INFLUENCE	_____
TIME	_____
SERVICE	_____
SPACE	_____
KNOWLEDGE	_____
COMMON SENSE	_____
GRATITUDE	_____
TOTAL	_____

If your total is less than 50, you need to develop a better understanding of what you have to offer. Look deeper. It is important that you have the proper respect for the trading cards that are always in your pocket. Once you learn to appreciate the assets which are yours and yours alone, you will have the wherewithal to get what you want, wherever you happen to be. And you won't have to have a large cash reserve to be able to do this, either.

As you read Part Two your cash on hand will Sstttretttch!!!

In this next section you will find *21 specific ways to save on almost anything.* So many price-cutting suggestions will be presented all at once that you may find it difficult to see ways to apply these purchasing plans at the first reading.

Do not worry about this. Read the section for pleasure. You

will absorb many of the principles subconsciously.[1] Later, when you are in a buying situation, you will find yourself putting one or more of the suggested plans to work.

You will find that most of the savings are explained in terms of *cash* savings. A few other trades are suggested, but it is our belief that if you realize what cash savings are available to you, you will find your own ways to make trades other than with cash.

---

[1] One, or even two, of the principles will make such immediate good sense to you that you will want to put the outlined plan to work in the next few days or weeks. Put a dollar bill as a book mark between the pages where the plan is explained. This will be a money-saving reminder the next time you open the book.

Part Two

21 specific ways to save on almost anything

1

Buy Wholesale

Buy an automobile wholesale and you save 25%; buy an overcoat this way and you save 45%; buy a dining room suite and you save at least 50%. The trick is to buy merchandise where your retailer buys.

The next time you are about to lay out a sizeable amount of money for a retail purchase, find out from your local library or chamber of commerce whether such merchandise is manufactured in your state. You may be able to save lots more than 30% by buying wholesale.

Buying direct from the wholesaler

There are two reasons why the wholesaler dislikes selling direct to the consumer. Retailers who buy from him resent his selling to *their* customers for prices less than they get; and, he is not geared to sell direct. Therefore, such selling is a nuisance.

The wholesaler may sell to 300 buyers, who in turn sell to 3,000,000 consumers or more. Now if 3,000,000 consumers suddenly descend on him, he will have to close his doors. So why would any wholesaler ever sell to the consumer?

The wholesaler's profit per item

The wholesaler's profit per item is as great when he sells to you as when he sells to a buyer for a retail store, so he has no immediate economic reason for not selling direct. But how do you reach him?

The one way is to seek out a wholesaler you know. Let's say your uncle manufactures raincoats. You can buy from his showroom wholesale.

Another way is to walk into a wholesaler cold and ask if you can buy direct. You have a 50-50 chance here, depending on your approach and on what person you talk to.[1]

Rule: *Go to the top.* Clerks in a showroom have to follow the rule laid down by the owner *not* to sell to someone coming in from the street. The owner made the rule; he can break it.

Approaches that make sense

If you can honestly say any of the following, you will get a break from the wholesaler.

(1) "Joe sent me."

You may not have an uncle who makes raincoats but you may have an uncle who buys raincoats. Take a note from him to the wholesaler. The trick in the "Joe sent me" approach is to name a "Joe" whose business has meaning to the wholesaler. Just any "Joe" won't do.

(2) "I'm going to use the merchandise in an advertisement or a publicity picture."

Cary Grant says that the world's best-dressed women can be seen on Fifth Ave. and 57th Street in New York City. We agree. There are two reasons for this. It is the location of Bergdorf Goodman, one of the country's finest specialty shops, and it is the "main drag" for high-priced advertising and publicity women. These women who write the ads, handle the accounts, or supervise the photographs seldom buy anything retail. It is just good business for a wholesaler to allow them to buy from his showroom. This insures further use of his merchandise in ads, TV commercials, editorials.

---

[1] We walked into a wholesale plumbing outfit near Pawling, New York and asked to buy plastic pipe. The boss hesitated, saying his retailers would object. Then, he asked "Where are you from?" We told him and he smiled, saying "I don't sell to any plumbers there anyway," and gave us the pipe.

If you are using anything in an ad (pottery in a tablesetting, an outdoor lighting fixture in a garden scene, clothing, a close-up of a watch) do not be bashful about asking for merchandise for your own use. You can buy all you want wholesale.

(3) "I need it for a party."

One time in New York we had a party for a young photographer and his wife who were leaving for Spain. We went to the Spanish Tourist Bureau and asked for a Spanish movie. The director came in person and showed the film. For the party we wanted a paella pan for cooking and serving Spain's favorite chicken, rice, and seafood dish. We went to a supply house and told the owner what we were looking for.

The wholesaler suggested a department store where we could buy the paella pan. We said "We will not buy at all if we have to pay a high price. So you are not cheating the department store." He eventually gave us the pan for three reasons: He had a *now or never* sale; he knew that we would be entertaining many potential customers for his merchandise; and as a full-blooded Spaniard, he became emotionally involved in our project.

(4) "I am not actually in the business, but my work is somehow related."

New York, New Orleans, San Francisco—many American cities —have antique shops with a sign in the window that says *To The Trade Only*. These dealers buy from private homes or at auctions. They sell to decorators and stores with departments specializing in antiques. They cannot compete with their decorators. Other than that, they have no reason not to sell to you.

Many times we have bought from these dealers, telling them truthfully that we were decorating an apartment for sublet purposes, converting a barn, doing a room that calls for a particular chandelier, pair of andirons, or mirror. We give them an excuse to sell to us.

(5) "I am a buyer for 'Blank and Blank.'"

If you have a friend who is entitled to buy wholesale, do not be bashful about using his card or letter of introduction. (He may even let you do some scouting for him.) The wholesaler may suspect that you are not a professional buyer, but he will not object to doing a favor for your friend.

There is one last way to get something wholesale, and that is simply to *ask*.

(6) "I wonder if you'd let me buy *one* of those hats, or sugar bowls, or boxes of candy."

One day our daughter noticed a handsome feathered hat in the window of a showroom. She walked in and said, "Is there any chance of my buying one of these hats?" The man said "Yes." And she walked out with a hat for which she paid $8. She later saw the same hat for $16.95.

Sometimes the direct approach works.

Disadvantages of buying wholesale

1. YOU CAN'T TRY ON THE MERCHANDISE.

When you buy clothing wholesale, you must know your size (and sizes from different manufacturers vary) and know what looks good on you. Merchandise can't be tried on.

2. YOU CAN'T RETURN THE MERCHANDISE.

Buy a raincoat from a wholesaler, and he will hand you a coat, packed just as he ships it to a store. Now, suppose you get this home and find the belt buckle is broken. You can't return the coat.

3. YOU HAVE TO PAY CASH.

When you buy wholesale, you pay cash unless you buy through one of the wholesaler's regular customers who will let you pay him.

The best way to buy wholesale

The best way to buy wholesale is to buy through a friend who is buying for a retail outlet. We have friends who own a specialty shop for women in southern Iowa. We like them, so when they come East to buy, they often stay with us. These fashion experts always report to us their opinion of Adele Simpson's line, Hannah Troy's, and Harvey Berin's. They tell us what Davidow's new suits are like, Ceil Chapman's ballgowns, dresses from Junior Sophisticates. And invariably, our guest says something like, "Wouldn't you like to have me get you a walking suit? Adele Simpson has a beautiful red one." Or "Don't you want me to pick up some dresses for the girls for Christmas? There's a silver sheath at Junior Sophisticates that would look great on Dina."

Luckily the girls and women in our family can wear size 10 or 12, or 5 or 7, as the case may be, and we buy knowing that nothing will have to be changed.

When our friends buy for us, they have the merchandise shipped with other purchases to their store. Then they ship to us. We pay the wholesale price, plus the shipping.

Wholesale buying through friends is a break, but it is hard to come by. You cannot ask a retail person to give you things wholesale as you can ask a wholesale person to give you things wholesale. The wholesaler makes a profit when he sells to you. The retailer does not. Therefore, another type of trade has to be made.

Men and women "in the trade" swap favors daily. The owner of a sporting goods shop lets a friend buy golf clubs wholesale; he in turn gets a refrigerator wholesale from his friend. The coat manufacturer lets the wife of a friend get a coat from the showroom; in turn, his wife gets an evening gown wholesale from the manufacturer across the street.

If you have no way of getting anything wholesale through your job, you cannot swap this way. You will have to make another kind of trade.

The trade that comes naturally

You may be entertaining a hardware salesman. Noticing that your lawn mower is not ship-shape he may say "I'm putting in an order for mowers tonight. Would you like one wholesale?"

Not long ago we took an executive of U. S. Rubber for a ride in our boat. We had a good time, and he said during the ride, "Say, we have a new fabric that would be great on the floor of this boat. Shall I get you some wholesale?"

Most friends who can get something for you wholesale are glad to accommodate.

Steps to take

Here are possible ways for you to get things wholesale.

Your work—are you a wholesaler, yourself, or a buyer or the manager of a retail store? You can set up a series of trades, so that you will seldom have to pay the retail price for anything.

Friends in business. This is a good way to get things wholesale for yourself, but you usually can't use this source to trade with others. Few retailers will sell wholesale to your friends.

Wholesale outlets in your own town. In your office building there may be a showroom for lampshades or globes or clocks. Your best approach is to ask the receptionist if she believes "Mr. Jones would let me buy a lampshade?" She will do your selling for you. You may know the local manufacturer who makes toys or ties or typewriters.

Too much trouble?

It takes less time to select a lampshade in a wholesale show-room than it does in the busy furniture department of a large store.

Wholesale buying is good discipline. You can't putter. You have to decide what you want and abide by that decision. And think of the saving! The only flaw is that once you buy wholesale, you will hate to pay the retail price for anything!

10 BASIC THINGS YOU CAN BUY AT A WHOLESALE PRICE WHEREVER YOU HAPPEN TO BE

(Here we refer to products sold before any mark-up is added.)

1. FRESH FOOD (including garden supplies, fruit, eggs, and milk)
   Buy direct from the grower or farmer. Or buy *with* a jobber or supplier who buys direct.[2]

2. PROCESSED FOODS (including canned goods, flour, sugar, butter, frozen foods)
   To buy direct, you may have to take seconds, work through a jobber friend, or buy with a group from a processor. Watch for come-ons at your store, which are often offered below wholesale.

3. MEATS (fresh, frozen or processed)
   Buy in quantity from a farmer, keep the meat in a freezer until needed. Sell off in sections to your friends. Or buy with a group from your local packer who may ship bacon, hams, frozen chickens, etc.

4. CHILDREN'S CLOTHING (including snowsuits, dresses, suits, socks, shoes, overshoes, hats, underwear, anything)
   Buy wholesale by going to the factory and offering to buy defective merchandise (a buttonhole may be outsize). Or make an arrangement with a friend who buys direct. (This takes a trade.)

5. WOMEN'S CLOTHING (including sweaters, dresses, lingerie, hats, coats, suits, shoes)
   Follow the rules for buying children's clothes. And watch for end-of-season sales for extreme clothes. These clothes, especially hats, are marked down below the wholesale price.

---

[2] When you buy from a jobber friend, let him make some profit—in fact, insist on it. Or, give in exchange a favor he finds attractive. That way you can go back again. This same buying rule applies when you're getting a car from a dealer, even if that dealer happens to be your brother-in-law.

6. MEN'S CLOTHES (including shoes, jackets, suits, hats, underwear, overcoats, sweaters, etc.)
   Ask a manufacturer for seconds. Seconds are usually close to
   first class quality. Or buy through a friend (store owner)
   who buys direct. Buy by mail from the maker.

7. BOOKS AND RECORDS AND TOYS.
   Books, records, and toys at discount houses are often priced
   below wholesale, as come-ons.

8. BAKED GOODS
   Buy bread and rolls no longer fresh.

9. FURNITURE
   Buy seconds from a local manufacturer, or watch for end-of-
   season sales where storage for large items like gliders, porch
   swings, etc., is a problem.

10. RUGS
    In a large city, go to an auction where left-over pieces of
    new rugs are sold. (They may have been left-over from the
    decorating of a new store or country club or restaurant.) In a
    small town, have your hooked rug made locally or watch for
    a sale of irregulars.

2

Go to a Discount Store

When times are good, merchants do not make price reductions, unless such price reductions lead to more profits. Some savings at discount stores are so dramatic you may ask "How can they do it?" Here's how: (1) By advertising cut rate prices, they attract more customers. With large volume selling they can afford to take less profit per item.[1] (2) Many are members of a chain or have a large enough business to buy in volume; therefore, they buy for less. (3) They push their own brands which are priced lower than national brands which have to absorb high advertising costs. (4) They often are located out of the high rent district.

The phony discount house has a ticket on each item with two prices. One is supposedly the regular price; one is the mark-down price. Too often, the regular price is inflated, and the discount price is really the regular price.

The legitimate discount store may have a list price and a mark-down price on each item. The difference is that the list price is the true selling price; the mark-down price is much lower than in any other store.

To tell whether the discount house near you is a good one, write down seven familiar items. Suggestion: a large size tube of toothpaste, aspirin, a large size jar of face cream, shaving cream, vitamins, facial tissues, perfume (a family member's favorite

---

[1] Sometimes, only the "loss leaders" are marked way down. Other prices are marked up. Either learn to spot the "loss leaders" and buy only these, or shop elsewhere.

brand). Check the price of each item in the cut rate store, a regular drug store, and the nearest large department store. Are five of the items priced lower at the cut-rate store? Fine! This is a good place to shop. You will get 20% off on many things, 30% off on some things, and 40% off on the *leaders*. The only trouble is you will be inclined to buy more than you need. (A giant bottle of shampoo which you will never use is no bargain even at 40% off.) *Don't buy everything in sight!*

There are ways to save 50% at a good cut rate drug store *if you read the labels.*

Federal drug laws specify that most of the drug products you buy be compounded to a USP (United States Pharmacopoeia) formula. If the label on a bottle of aspirin says that this product is compounded to USP specifications, buy with confidence, no matter what the brand. Do not pay for a name, even though the advertising stresses *integrity*.

Few multi-vitamin tablets are manufactured by the company with its name on the bottle. A manufacturer compounds vitamin tablets according to USP specifications. Then this manufacturer *sells* these tablets to many different drug houses, each one of which advertises the *identical* vitamin tablets in his own way. Learn to *look through* advertising and packaging when you are buying drugs and/or cosmetics.

Read the list of ingredients on the cosmetics you buy. Often only the fragrance makes one after-shave lotion or bath oil or shampoo different from another. (Some theatrical creams are odorless. Often they can be purchased for as much as 25 cents an ounce less than perfumed creams which have ingredients that are identical.)

We have an elegant friend who buys theatrical cleansing cream in large quantities. She removes some of the cream from its giant jar, swirls in a drop of Nina Ricci perfume, then puts it into a Wedgwood jar on her dressing table. (The French perfume she buys by mail for more than 30% off; the Wedgwood jar she found at an auction.) Her lovely jar of scented cream costs her less than a jar of face cream at Woolworth's.

Whenever a store brand and a highly advertised brand contain exactly the same ingredients, *buy the store brand.*

Note: Get to know your pharmacist. Not long ago we took ours a prescription for one of our parents. He told us that we did not need a prescription. In checking the ingredients of the name brand of iron tablets our doctor was ordering, we found that they were identical to a less expensive brand. Did our parent need the tablets? Was the doctor ordering the pills to give his patient a psychological lift? Always ask if you really *need* the prescription to buy a particular product. If not, you are overpaying at a drug store and at the doctor's office, too.

Other discount items

Watches, cameras, home appliances, TV sets, blankets, air-conditioning units—all kinds of things are sold at discount houses. Check the prices of an electric blanket, a vacuum cleaner, a TV set at a department store, a nearby appliance store, and at your discount store. Are the prices lower on these items at the discount place? If the quality is the same on these items, buy there with confidence.

Lower than wholesale

One night when our cut-rate drugstore was closed, we went to a regular store to buy some witch hazel. The druggist charged us 79 cents. We said "At the discount house this is only 59 cents." "Then, the guy is making less than a penny a bottle," the druggist said. "This bottle cost me 58 cents. I don't know how he does it!"

He does it by selling so much witch hazel that he gets a better price than 58 cents when he buys. Also, he takes less profit per bottle.

Less than wholesale

Sometimes a discount store sells an item for less than what the competitor has to pay wholesale. The store takes a loss to build its reputation for selling top merchandise at a low price. Books and records at many discount stores are the *loss leaders*.

Big savings

Some lumber yards operate like discount stores. You pay cash and carry home your own purchases. It's worth it. You can get more than 40% off on standard size windows, doors, boards, and other supplies.

Rule for comparison shopping

Once your store check proves your discount place is a good one, forget about comparison shopping on small items. But do check three stores when your purchase will exceed $75. Saving on a range or a power mower or shingles for your roof is well worth an afternoon on the town. Also, to compete with discount stores, department stores push their own "loss leaders"—especially in their bargain basements.

Buy Second Hand

A woman buys a black alligator bag at Lord & Taylor's for $250; a week later she dies. Her personal effects are sold to a dealer who sells the bag for $75.

You buy bookshelves for $95. A month later half your house is blown away by a hurricane. You remodel without using the shelves. You can't get more than 50% of your purchase price for the shelves, if that much.

You buy a Ford sedan for $3200. The next month you are transferred to Japan. Even though your car has not been driven any more than the new cars at your dealer's, you can't realize much more than $2500 on it.

Used merchandise is marked-down merchandise.

Who used it?

The person who has never bought anything but new merchandise may cringe at the thought of buying anything that another person has used.

Let's say you see a good-looking sports jacket for your college son in a men's store for $49.95. In a second hand store you see the same style sports jacket for $14. It shows no wear.

There may be two factors that will keep you from buying. (1) Your son may feel uncomfortable in a second hand jacket. (2) You may be concerned for health reasons. We hope you can tell your son that you picked up a jacket for $14 that is selling across the street for about $50. If not, you may have to tell him a white lie. A few years from now (when he grows up a little) you can tell him where you got the jacket.

Naturally, you don't want to gamble with your son's health. But if you buy him a *new* jacket, it undoubtedly has been tried on by strangers, and later it will be tossed into cleaning fluid with other clothes at the cleaner's.

The second hand jacket will have been cleaned. (In many cases, clothes in second hand stores still bear the cleaning label.)

When merchandise is being sold for the 10th, 12th, or 20th time, no one worries about the health angle. We recently watched a college girl don a Colonial ballgown for a costume ball which she found in an antique shop. A week later this same girl rejected an evening gown in a resale shop. "I don't know who has worn it," she said.

Health laws in most states prevent buyers from buying mattresses second hand (they can accept them as gifts, but they cannot buy them); also, from buying overstuffed furniture which has not been disinfected. We are all for this. But once furniture is disinfected, blankets and sheets have been washed, and clothing has been cleaned, we are all for picking up a bargain.

Three things to think about
when buying second-hand clothing

1. What am I going to use this for?
2. Why was it sold?
3. How much did this dealer pay for it? (Get this in mind, and you will know how far you can dicker.)

When buying children's blue jeans, slacks, sweaters and underwear, consider the wear that you will get. (Clothes which have obviously been laundered over and over again are not a good buy for you.) When you need a costume for a Halloween party, you want the most unusual costume you can find. Long wear does not need to enter your mind.

When buying a dress suit or a glamorous ball gown, wear is

not something you have to be too concerned about. You want evening clothes that are basically correct—and *becoming*.

The last owner

For children, you want clothes that have been outgrown, not outworn. (We picked up a little French-embroidered coat in a resale shop. A good buy, the coat was (1) imported, and (2) not worn at all. We surmised it was purchased for one Easter, outgrown by the next.)

An adult sells clothes because (1) he may have gained or lost weight; (2) he may be extremely style-conscious so he doesn't like a last year's suit; (3) he may be an actor who wears special clothes for every part; (4) she may be in the trade so she cannot wear clothes a second time; (5) or he or she may be dead or dead broke. Such clothes are always inexpensive, but remember the dealer pays *something* for the clothes, so he will not give them away.

Keep in mind that the dealer (1) wants to make a sale; (2) is a past master at wheeling and dealing; (3) is not going to sell for less than *he* paid.

One cardinal rule

Whether you are buying a mink coat or a car or a love seat or anything else, obey this one rule: *Know Your Merchandise.* If you see a leopard muff in a second hand store and you don't know a Somali from a fake fur, you are out over your head! The same holds true of everything. How can you make a good deal on a used Castro Convertible if you don't know what a new one should cost? How can you buy a good used Cadillac if you haven't priced this year's model? How can you buy a second hand set of English bone china dinnerware if you don't know retail costs?

As an expert you have two advantages: (1) You know your merchandise and (2) the dealer knows you know.

If you are not an expert, *find* an expert. When you are buying furs, the expert can be a retired furrier, a former fashion editor, a wealthy intelligent woman who has owned many furs, a breeder, a former personal shopper. (Don't expect a hard-working dealer, furrier, or breeder to go shopping with you without pay. The retired expert, on the other hand, may be flattered to be consulted and may be delighted to help you for nothing.)

Don't buy anything that doesn't fit your needs. (A beaded Dior gown may be a great bargain in your second-hand shop—but may look ludicrous on you.)

Two times to buy second hand merchandise

The two times to go after second hand clothes or furniture or anything else are (1) when you need to make a major purchase but do not want to pay the full retail price and (2) when you want to make a lot of purchases for a specific project.

You may need a second car for occasional driving, an evening coat for one party, a playpen for one week. Buy second hand. If you want to furnish a summer cottage in a few days, go to a second hand store for studio couches, double decker beds, chests of drawers, and tables and chairs.

What can you buy second hand?

You can buy everything second hand that you can buy first hand. Want a camera? A suit? Skis? In the classified section of your telephone book, look up *Second-Hand Stores.* Or look under the name of the merchandise. (Ex. *Automobile Dealers*—Used Cars.) Look under *Merchandise Offerings* in your newspaper classifieds. Radios, office furniture, rugs, electrical appliances, hydraulic presses, men's suits, ice cream freezers, all are often advertised.

You usually pay less when buying from a dealer than from an individual. Individuals are sentimental, dealers are realistic. They buy from desperation sellers, price their merchandise at whatever they think you will pay.

Pawnshops

Look in the classified directory under *Pawnbrokers* for some of the best sources of second hand cameras, diamonds, guns, musical instruments and, sometimes, articles of clothing. The trick in buying unredeemed merchandise [1] from a pawnbroker is to know what the cost of the merchandise is *new*. Then when you spot the camera or guitar or gun you want in a shop, you know a bargain when you see it. The usual saving, if you know what you're about, is 30% to 50%.

Antiques

Antique dealers are different from second-hand dealers. They are specialists. So you pay more for the merchandise.

The trick is to spot a rare antique at a second-hand store. Or to identify a great painting at a warehouse sale. Or to pick up some of Napoleon's dinnerware at a country attic sale.

How to spot a treasure

Thank your lucky stars if you were born with taste! You won't buy junk because you don't react to poor workmanship, color combinations that are "off," bad design, shoddiness. The woman with good taste knows how to use a vivid blue scarf, a beaded evening bag from the 20's, a cameo. She doesn't always care if something is authentic. But it must be *effective*.

Even if you have good taste you will not come home with a treasure unless you are an expert. If you have made a study of lace, you will be more apt to find an exquisite treasure in the bottom of a trunk than will your unknowing neighbor. If you know French history, you will know whether a gold cupid offered for sale in a small hotel could possibly have graced Richelieu's drawing room, as is claimed. If you have hunted in Africa, you

---

[1] In some cities all unredeemed merchandise is sold from one Unredeemed Pledge Store; in others, from the same stores where the merchandise was pawned. Check a pawnshop in your town for your local ruling.

will not buy the head of an American buffalo believing it to be a Cape Buffalo.

Treasures have four characteristics: (1) excellent workmanship; (2) good overall form; (3) rarity; (4) historical significance. Use this checklist. You may find a treasure yet. And certainly you will dress better and have a more beautiful home if you do not insist that everything you buy be brand spanking new.

4

Call the Salvation Army

Many persons think of the Salvation Army as a place to give to, not to buy from. Don't overlook this way to get good furniture at rock bottom prices. Sophisticated antique dealers do not forget this source. A New York Brigadier told us that when a load comes in to one of the city's big S.A. stores from an old home, antique dealers are waiting at the store for the truck.

Decorators, as well as antique dealers, keep their eyes on the Salvation Army stores, so do second-hand dealers. So do stage designers and bright young fashion girls on the lookout for accessories for an ad or a window display.

Salvation Army procedure

When you call the Salvation Army to take away newspapers, rugs, furniture, clothes, kitchen equipment or anything else, a truck comes for whatever you want to get rid of. Newspapers and rags are sold to a dealer; furniture, clothing and equipment are mended, refinished, and placed in a Salvation Army store. Proceeds of the sale of the merchandise is used for rehabilitation.

If your telephone directory lists no local store, ask your long distance operator for the number of the nearest Salvation Army center. You will be surprised at the prices. And if you live where old furniture has been allowed to accumulate in attics, you can find beautiful things.

Most people contribute to the Salvation Army at moving time

73

or after a death in the family, or at a time of a divorce or when
new furnishings are coming in and old things have to be disposed
of. The person disposing of something considers it of little worth.
This may be just what you are looking for.

What to buy

Any Salvation Army store has all kinds of chests, chairs, tables,
beds, dressers, cupboards, lamps, pictures, and rugs.

The better your taste the more you can put these things to use
in your home. Maybe you will throw away the pictures you buy
and keep the frames, cut down the library table for a coffee table,
or antique [1] the old chest of drawers.

One couple we know bought an outsize secretary for $12.
They removed the upper shelves and hung them on brackets for
books. They made the base into a toy chest for their little girl.
The wood scroll from the top is now mounted over the head of
their bed. Two gold satin curtains (bought there for $5) are
swagged back from the scroll to give a Louis XVI feeling to their
bedroom. A home furnished with imagination can be more
dramatic when furnished with Salvation Army furniture than
when furnished with mass produced suites.

Basics

Not only the poor buy basic furniture at the Salvation Army.

A friend who has a large home with 14 acres of land hires a
college boy to help her. Three summers ago she furnished two
rooms for her "gardener" over her garage with a sofa, chairs,
lamps, desk, television set, bed, and dresser from the Salvation
Army.

Look for children's things there. In many homes when a playpen, crib, high chair, and infant clothing are outgrown, parents
call "Sally's."

---

[1] Paint article with white paint and rub in gold paint. Put on new knobs which
you can buy at a store that sells decorative hardware.

This year columnist Mike Royko reported from Chicago: "Salvation Army stores are about the biggest sellers of clothing in Chicago. There is no shortage of persons trying to stretch a wholesale income into retail possessions. In a year, the outlet stores with the red shields that dot Chicago will sell at least 750,000 items of clothing. The big demand—certainly during the back-to-school rush—is for children's clothes. Even for used clothes, they are bargain priced. Girls' coats have a top cost of $2.50. Dresses are 35 cents to a dollar. Boys' jackets go up to $1.50. Shoes are a buck."

Merchandise is priced low so that men and women with low incomes will not have to do without a bed or a sofa or a rug as they need it. But money from sales of this kind cannot begin to do the job the agency has set out to do. Your business is welcomed.

A personal experience

With the landlord's permission, we once rented *two* apartments, one above the other, in a town house on 61st street in New York. We paid $125 for the upstairs apartment which had a large "porch," $250 for the downstairs apartment which had a 60 foot garden. So for $375 we had a duplex with upstairs and downstairs fireplaces, upstairs and downstairs baths, and upstairs and downstairs terraces. We had two bedrooms, a large living room and a large kitchen and all kinds of closet space. This space and arrangement was unheard of in this neighborhood at this rental.

Our aim was to furnish the apartment from top to bottom, including carpets, draperies, kitchen equipment, everything, for less than $2,000. We did, and handsomely, with the help of the Salvation Army.

Except for dull gold draperies which we bought at an auction for $6 and our hi fi equipment, which we bought wholesale, our total outlay for our living room was about half as much as what most of our friends paid that year for a sofa.

What's more, our living room was dramatic enough to be described as sensational in a special two-column decorator story in the New York Herald Tribune.

Here is the inventory of the furniture in our living room.

19th century spinet desk	$ 5.00
Barrel-back desk chair	7.00
Beige velvet chair with matching chaise footstool	27.00
Blue velvet club chair	16.00
Important oak drop-leaf table	40.00
Marble top end table (c. 1890)	25.00
Crystal chandelier	32.00
Italian "library table" which we painted black, cut down for a coffee table	12.00
3-tiered end table	6.00
2 dozen 24-inch square mirrors which we put up on the wall around the fireplace ($2.00 each)	48.00
Small black waist high chest with doors (which we used to house our hi fi)	12.00
Plain carved green carpet which we cut down and used as wall to wall carpeting	27.00
One violin and bow (for wall decoration)	2.00
One shoji screen (which we lined with plexiglass and hung from ceiling as light fixture)	16.00
Small French andirons	14.00
Two camel saddles (which we used as fireside chairs)	31.00
One green striped silk love seat	40.00
One ocelot skin (which we strung on bamboo strips)	18.00
3 large cylindrical lamps with fabric shades	36.00
Total	$414.00

When we went away from the apartment to Europe for three months, we sublet the duplex for $800 a month. While we were away, the building was sold to an investor. He in turn wanted to sell the building, so he paid us $2500 not to renew our option at the end of our three year lease. We actually *sold* our apartment to the landlord we were renting from. (Everyone who considered buying the building wanted to live in the duplex.) Our Salvation Army home was a good investment.

5

Go to an Auction

The Romans sold the spoils of war at auction. The English long have sold real estate this way. The Dutch sell their tulips at auction. Auctions are accepted around the world.

During the past three centuries, Americans have bought tobacco, land, livestock, hides, and even slaves at auction. Today, farms, art collections, furniture, rugs, and bric-a-brac are sold this way. There is not a community in America where the auction is not respected as a solid way of doing business.

Look at the New York Times some Sunday in Section 9 for everything from paintings to restaurant equipment. Look at the New York Herald Tribune any day, and you will find a page devoted to auctions for everything from toilet bowls (at a plumbing supply auction) to poolside chairs (at an auction of furnishings of a defunct Country Club). Look in any paper any day anywhere in the United States, and you will see an auction notice.

Auctioneers operate in one of two ways:

(1) They buy up all the contents of a house or a business for a given price. Then they auction off the items piece by piece;

or—

(2) They take merchandise on a consignment basis, agreeing to pay the person selling a piano, a horse or a car, a given percentage of whatever the item brings.

To buy wisely from an experienced auctioneer, you have to resist buying emotionally.

Three things to do before bidding at an auction

Follow these rules and you will not run into trouble.

1. Inspect the merchandise before the auction.

2. Decide what items you are interested in and find out what these items are sold for elsewhere.

3. Write down the absolute *tops* you will pay for each item.

Examine each item for mended places, cracks, non-working parts, and other flaws. Do your own appraising before the sale, and you will avoid being surprised by something on the auction bloc which may capture your attention momentarily but is something you have no use for.

In large cities, merchandise is exhibited by professional auctioneers two or three days before the auction. At court auctions, the sale is announced in the local paper before the appointed day, so you can inspect the buildings or walk the land. Contents of homes to be auctioned in small towns or fund-raising auctions are advertised to give you time to look over what is being sold before the sale begins.

Do comparison shopping. You may find at an auction a delicate Dresden doll that will look like a dream in your daughter's Cecil Beaton-inspired dressing room. See this at an exhibit before an auction, and you can look into a few shop windows to see what a doll like this sells for retail. See this doll for the first time in an auctioneer's hand, and you will overbid.

At a farm auction, you may see a small pickup truck that is just what you want. It is obvious that inspection of this in advance makes for wiser buying.

Make up your mind before you make your *first* bid how high you will go with your *last* bid. If you write this figure down, and stick to this figure, you will have no worries. More often than not you will get the auctioned merchandise for far less than you have told yourself you will pay.

You can get great buys at auctions, better buys, usually, than you can get at second hand stores, and far better buys than you can get at antique shops. At one auction, you will see local antique dealers. Next time you see the auctioned items in their stores, the prices will have gone up.

(Example: At an auction on Long Island, where the furnishings from an estate were sold, we bought two round 12-inch white Copenhagen plaques, one perfect, one mended, for $7.00. A dealer at the same auction bought a second pair, both perfect, for $14. Two weeks later in New York we saw the pair he bought in his Madison Avenue antique shop. The price for the pair was now $100.)

Unusual pieces

Auctions, even more than Salvation Army stores, are wonderful sources for out-of-the-ordinary things. At one, you will find a Sheraton style bed with a canopy; at another, a Pennsylvania Dutch painted pine cupboard; at still another, a mahogany console table.

Some days will be lucky days. You will see at an exhibition some handsome brass antique curtain tiebacks; at the same place, an old English wall cupboard with seat and arms attached; perhaps, an Italian sideboard buffet. Bid wisely, and you can bring them all home for $68.00.

Your home will take on character the more you buy at auctions.

All kinds of auctions

We bought a Chinese chest at an auction for $23 which now houses our FM radio and hi fi set. We have found exotic lamps at auctions and once bought four beautiful fabric lampshades for a dollar. One day we bought unusual draperies made of hand-blocked linen for $12 a pair. We bought a framed Picasso print at a Connecticut auction for $3.00, linen wastebaskets at a Pennsylvania auction for 50 cents apiece, a custom made Victorian style Castro at a New York auction for $9 which we had covered for $125 and which is now the pride of our parlor. One day we went to an automobile auction at Roosevelt Raceway with a dealer friend of ours and bought a two-year old Renault car for $185.[1]

The most amusing thing we ever found at an auction was an old French pianola. (This has pedals like a player piano, but it has no keys. It was made to be *mounted* on a regular piano.) With it, we got a large chest full of player piano rolls. We paid $28 for our purchase, and two days later we sold the pianola for $85. We kept the rolls.

Our interest in the pianola led to our reading about the cutting of player piano rolls. We found that Gershwin used to cut rolls for $25 per roll, and later, Fats Waller cut some for $100 a roll. We decided that rolls hung on the wall as *scrolls* would make unusual Americana-type decorations.

> (*Note from Cle:* Utilizing early jazz instruments, the banjo, saxophone, and piano keys, I painted jazz designs on two rolls, similar to the ones cut by Gershwin and Waller. I backed up the cut paper with black hot iron mending tape. We named one scroll "Jazz" and the other "Ragtime," and hung the pair in our studio. The first week a manufacturer from the middlewest bought the pair of scrolls for $200. Some day we will merchandise the rest of the rolls in our chest as "Piano Roll Scrolls.")

Money-saving tricks

1. Do not buy a painting at auctions where dealers are bidding for paintings. At such auctions we buy what other customers *don't* want. It was at a sale at New York's Plaza Auction Galleries where everyone was bidding on paintings that we bought our Castro for $9.00. (The auction had taken the Castro along with other furnishings from an estate in order to get the paintings in the house.) That same Castro at a gallery appealing to buyers from a *lower* income bracket would have gone for at least $100.

---

[1] We paid the dealer $50 for taking us with him.

2. Bid with restraint. Enthusiasm attracts other bidders. Do not call out your bids. Raise your hand.

3. When an item is obviously going for an exceptionally low price, *buy* even though you may not have planned to buy this item before the bidding started.

4. Buy big items at an auction. (An auctioneer has to empty his gallery before his next shipment comes in. A massive hand carved dining room suite and 12 chairs just can't stay around.)

5. Unless the exterior design is superb (a grandfather's clock) don't buy something that doesn't work. That $35 telescope on a tripod may cost you $150 to fix up; the $3 desk clock may cost you a repair job of $50.

6. Court auctions are the quickest, easiest, and safest way to buy anything. (Titles have to be cleared before the court can put property up for auction.) Watch your newspaper for legal notices where court auctions are announced.

It was at an auction of the probate court that we bought our 50-acre farm plus a barn and a house for $18,000. In less than a week we were offered more than this for half the land. You can get great buys at auctions.

Post Office auctions

The 15 Dead Parcel Post Branches of the U.S. Postal Service regularly hold auctions of "dead parcel post." [2] Mr. Marcel Vax, supervisor at the St. Paul, Minnesota, branch gave us this story of the auctions.

> Our branch, which disposes of dead parcel post from Minnesota, North and South Dakota, Wisconsin, and Upper Michigan, has an auction every month. We open all dead packages and divide into lots all merchandise to be auctioned. We may have one lot of men's shoes, another of

[2] Unclaimed packages which have been held more than 60 days.

transistor radios, another of small appliances, etc.—and will
sell 100 lots at a given sale. Bids for a lot usually start at $1.00.
At an average auction, we will have three or four second-
hand dealers and 200 or more average people looking for a
good buy.

If you want to attend these auctions in your part of the country
(perhaps, in your city), write to the Dead Letter Branch nearest
you [3] and ask to be put on the mailing list. Ten days before an
auction you will be sent an Auction Brochure. Get to the auction
an hour ahead of time. Opened packages will be on display.

---

[3] Your P.O. can tell you where.

6

Buy at a Thrift Shop

The Nearly New Shop at 802 Ninth Avenue in New York City is a cooperative venture of nine different New York social service or charitable agencies. One organization that takes part is a Wellesley Alumnae group, another is a missionary society, another is a visiting nurses' association.

The nine organizations pay for a director who knows when the store will open, what to do with donated merchandise, where things should be stored, etc. Volunteers from the various charities serve as markers and saleswomen.

Say a box containing a hand-crocheted bedspread, costume jewelry, two or three men's suits, and six pairs of shoes comes in. The marker puts the name of the donor in a book and after it the name of the charity which will get proceeds from the box. The same marker tags each item with the price she thinks it will bring, codes it with her notes in the book for proper credit.

The merchandise is then sent to the floor. Jewelry and small bric-a-brac go into the front window or center counter. Books and china go on special wall shelves. Clothes go on floor racks or are sent to the boutique. As in all Thrift Shops, the marker discards clothing marked with perspiration stains and/or spots and stains of other kinds.

The boutique at the Nearly New Shop is kept locked. In it are donated suits from Paris, furs (we saw a mink stole last time we were there in excellent condition marked at $40), and designer-made evening gowns.

Recently, a friend told us about a Thrift Shop in a small town in Vermont run by a local church organization.

"The markers for that Thrift Shop are the best dressed women in town," she said.

The marker not only has first choice of the merchandise that comes in, she can also mark the merchandise at whatever price she wants to pay.

Volunteers are not only honest, but overly so, but still they can put a realistic price on a cashmere sweater or pair of ski pants or a tiny Czechoslovakian vase and be the first to buy it *and still do right by the store* for this reason of policy: *Markers in all Thrift Shops are urged to err (if they must err) in the direction of marking too low, not too high, because Thrift Shops to succeed must maintain a reputation for great bargains!*

The trick of getting a bargain in a Thrift Shop is to recognize one when you see it. You can't tell anything from the price. Occasionally, you can talk to one of the volunteer saleswomen who is better informed, usually, than paid saleswomen in a store selling low-priced merchandise. She may tell you where the item came from.

Not long ago in a Thrift Shop, we saw a spool of lace—probably five yards in all—marked at 75 cents. It looked handmade. One of the saleswomen said, "It came in a box from Dina Merrill." Now Dina Merrill's mother has one of the finest collections of lace in America, so we bought. The lace is now stitched onto the bodice of a silk slip our daughter, Gwen, made for herself. The slip looks like a $49 Dior import.

One day, a conscientious marker for one of the participating societies at the Nearly New Shop opened a carton of miniatures— tiny glass chests, vases, candlesticks—which she believed had exceptional value. She took them up to the Sandwich Glass Museum near her home on Cape Cod and sold them. The money went to the Nearly New Shop. The other tiny pieces in the collection she marked for sale at the shop. Someone got a tremendous buy when these pieces went out to the center counter. Experts say the collection was an important one.

A marker at a shop in Illinois told us that she opened a collection of unusual-looking costume jewelry at the shop where she was donating time. The pieces were so handsome, she took them home to her husband who is an executive in a leading Chicago firm. At one glance, he offered her $75 for the collection, a price which she would have thought excessive at the shop. She sold it, returning the money to the cashier of the shop for credit to her own charity. The executive gave each secretary in his organization an unusual pin or bracelet or pair of earrings on *National Secretaries Day*. Naturally, he made a hit! "Always sent each one a rose before," he said. "This was something new."

You will find good buys at a Thrift Shop because it is the reputation for good buys that keeps a good shop going. If items do not sell the first day, they are sent back to the markers for re-pricing. Thus, in an enterprising, money-making shop, items are quickly sold and more merchandise is moved to the floor.

Remember, stock is donated at a Thrift Shop. Families that can afford to donate clothes and other possessions before they wear out usually pay more for such merchandise in the first place. So you get good quality.

7

Use Mail Order

There are two advantages other than convenience to ordering by mail. (1) You can get merchandise not sold in your home town stores; and (2) you can buy for less.

There are disadvantages. You often must wait for weeks for merchandise, especially when ordering from overseas. You cannot always be sure that you will receive exactly what you have in mind. There is usually no way to get your money back.

Follow this formula and you will save money and frustration.

Three Point Formula

1. Facts
   and
2. Costs—
   then,
3. Sit

1. Get the *facts* about the merchandise itself.

2. Compare the cost of the merchandise with similar merchandise sold retail. Check with the Customs Department, if you are ordering from overseas, to see what duty you will have to pay. Check the Postal Department (if you're ordering a large item C.O.D.) for postal charges.

3. Once you send in your order be prepared to sit and wait. (Don't order from overseas in October expecting to get merchandise to mail for Christmas.)

Follow this formula and you can save more than 30% and get some fabulous buys.

Elizabeth Squire, author of *The Mail Order Shopping Guide,* lists 800 American and foreign firms from which you can order beautiful and/or exotic specialties.

Here is an example from her book (*Permission M. Barrows and Company*).

> The Thai Silk Co., 311/6-7 Suriwongse Road, Box 906, G.P.O., Bangkok, Thailand. *Catalogue free.* The extraordinarily beautiful and colorful hand-woven Siamese silks that can be sent to you from this Bangkok firm are among the best buys in the world. Prices for 40 inch widths in either plain colors or exciting stripes and checks (some hot pinks and purples, others muted greys, blues, or browns) range from $3.60 to $5.00 a yard. Postage for the average order comes to about $2.50 and duty to 32%. These exquisite silks in Manhattan are priced at $17, and higher, a yard. Samples of the material are mailed on request. Also brocades in silk or metallic thread for $5.50 to $10.00 a yard. Specify which materials you want when requesting samples.

Following the *Facts* formula, here's how to get the silk (for a theatre suit, perhaps) with satisfaction guaranteed.

1. FACTS: Send for samples. Compare the samples with silks in local stores.

2. COSTS: How does the cost compare? Let's say that if you buy the two yards at the store you will pay $34 plus tax for the silk. If you buy from Thailand, you will pay, at $3.60 a yard, $7.20 for the silk. Your postage will be $2.50. Your duty will be $2.30. For the two yards you will pay $12 rather than $34.

   THEN: Send a check for $7.20 (or $9.70 to include $2.50 for postage, if the package is not to come C.O.D.) Your duty will not be included. The exact duty will be established when your package comes through customs.[1]

3. SIT: Wait until the package arrives via parcel post. Your postman will deliver the package and collect the duty (of approximately $2.30 in this case) at your door. Be ready with cash.

Mail order in this country

Mail order bloomed in rural areas of the United States in the late 1800's for three practical reasons: (1) America was a vast country with a great rural population; (2) this farm population was hungry for merchandise sold in cities; (3) our postal system had expanded with the railroads. Farm wives could order from a catalogue and get corsets, long underwear, hat pins, diapercloth, baby bottles, high button shoes—anything they could think of— within weeks. No wonder the Montgomery Ward and Sears Roebuck catalogues were standard equipment in rural homes.

Sears and Montgomery Ward today do not beam their catalogues to farmers, only. They offer Italian designed dresses, antiques, and even great paintings. Many Americans are now ordering by mail, not because they can't get into the stores, but because they like to shop by mail.[2]

---

[1] There is a customs regulation stating that parcels of less than $10 value sent as gifts may pass through customs duty free. So some merchandise you order may not be charged duty, even though you will not specify *gift* when ordering. Sometimes, the shipper stamps "unsolicited gift" on the package. There are so many abuses of the "gift regulation" customs officers tell us the regulation will eventually have to be changed. In the meantime, your overseas parcels may come duty-free. Inspectors let many parcels come through free because the cost for evaluating every piece of merchandise would cost more than the revenue it would produce. Do not be surprised if you pay no duty, but do not depend on its coming in free, either.

[2] Catalogue merchandise is marked about 10% lower than store merchandise, sometimes more. (Example—water skis in Sears' catalogue, $14; in the Danbury store, $20.) At the end of the season, when stores are clearing the floor of seasonal merchandise, store prices may be lower than catalogue prices. Sears' policy is not to lower a store price to correspond with the catalogue price on customer demand. "That would knock out mail order completely," said one manager.

Here are five types of merchandise you can buy by mail:

1. Basic merchandise like men's workclothes, women's aprons, children's playclothes, etc.

2. Novelties like hand-carved wooden whistles for children, drinking glasses from around the world, unusual mobiles, etc.

3. Imports like hand-smocked baby clothes from Paris, petit-point bags from Austria, ships' models from Denmark.

4. The old standbys like books, art pieces, seeds, and records.

5. Food and beverages.

To order from some houses, you have to pay a membership fee; sometimes, you have to pay for a catalogue. When a new catalogue is issued (the Sears and Ward catalogues come out every six months) you usually have to order $10 worth of merchandise before you are eligible for a new book.

Here are the addresses of three houses where you can get information about catalogues:

Montgomery Ward & Co., 393 7th Avenue, New York City

Sears Roebuck & Company, 360 West 31st Street, New York City

Spiegel, Box 8282, Philadelphia, Pa. 19101 (another giant!)

Novelties

For novelties, read editorial announcements as well as advertisements. Read the "What's New" columns in women's service magazines, newspaper stories about new products, regional folders. Read the Personal Column in the classified section, small display ads in special magazines like Popular Mechanics and in the Sunday newspaper. Here are things you will begin to see: Small cast iron Moby Dick, $1.00 when ordered from the Mystic Seaport Stores, Mystic, Conn.; old sap buckets painted with fruit in bright colors from the Vermont North Country Store, Middletown, New Jersey; Bayberry Candle, $1, Sunset

House, Beverly Hills, Calif. We order novelties constantly for inclusion in Christmas and birthday boxes.

Of all the values you can get through mail order, the best are those that come from foreign countries. Send to Paris for perfume, Ireland for linen, England for woolens, Italy for silks. Take your choice of products around the world that have been perfected by residents of a particular place for generations.

It costs less to order direct from a foreign country than if you bought this same merchandise from an importer. The importer pays the same duty you pay, plus shipping costs and taxes. Be your own importer.

Here is an example. In Paris, Gladys Capras, editor of *La Note de Paris*, told us about an artist named Line Vautrin who had perfected a process for making picture frames out of bits of colored glass set in material of her own composition. The frames sparkle, taking nothing from a painting but providing a subtle complement.

With Gladys and Maurine Pestchansky, women's director in Paris of Sabena Airlines, we went to Miss Vautrin's home in a fifth floor apartment at 29 Quai des grands Augustius, Paris VI, overlooking the Seine. There Madame Vautrin carefully manipulated the dial of an old-fashioned safe, took out a precious Rouault, which she had just framed in a border of lustrous browns and reds. (Picasso sends Madame Vautrin paintings to be framed. Her frames also border Derain's paintings and others loved by the French.)

If you want a frame, you have to write to her, tell her about your painting, and ask her what her price will be for making a frame. Then send her the painting (insured, of course) and she will frame and return it. Prices range in the neighborhood of $400.

We know few who will send for a hand-made frame for a painting. But we did believe our readers might like a less expensive creation by Line Vautrin.

She offered us one—a doorknob to be mailed for $10, postage included. Send Miss Vautrin a sketch of a *door* for the room for which you want a doorknob. Tell her the dominant decorating color in the room. She will make a doorknob for you and send it to the person you designate for a total charge of $10. (Send your personal check the day you send the sketch and color preference.)

We include this little story, because it illustrates our point that mail order can bring truly exciting merchandise from overseas—and for little cost, too. Order from overseas. Get Waterford Crystal from Ireland, cashmere knitwear from London, diamonds from Belgium.[3]

Collect names of firms that will ship here. In Florence, a shopkeeper told us that he had just received an order from a California senator for 50 pure silk ties lined with silk. Shrewd senator! The cost, $1.50 per tie.

Look for mail order offers in the seat pockets of planes. This is mail order at its easiest. "A play kit for the little girl who wants to play stewardess. Write down her name and address, make out a check for $2.00, seal self-mailer and hand to stewardess. Your kit will be delivered." In a TWA plane we found an offer for a set of eight glasses with an emblem from a different country printed on each one. They were delivered to our home before we returned. In Europe we found a coupon for ordering duty-free liquor. The order went to Tourists International, Geneva, Switzerland. We declared the liquor when we returned, found the liquor at home. (Typical savings: 1 fifth of Piper Heidsieck, $3.98; the same champagne at our local liquor store, $9.70. The catch is you have to order it from outside of the United States.)

Mail order is an easy way to send gifts. Not only can the gifts be exotic but the wrapping is done for you. One shop which makes a specialty of this kind of mailing is Oberon at 73 Champs Elysees, Paris, France. (Catalogue .90 which will be credited to your first order.) You can order Dior lingerie, Lalique glass swans and

---

[3] A brochure from Joachim Goldenstein's Diamond Club, Antwerp, Belgium, tells us the 10% U. S. duty on imported diamonds is charged, but local taxes are not charged on the imported diamonds. Price comparison: U. S. Retail Price for an unmounted top-grade diamond, 2 carats in size—$4200; Antwerp 2 carat Emerald Cut Diamond AAA 1—$2249. All diamonds from Belgium are appraised by government appraisers before the package is sealed.

other figures, hand-smocked baby and children's clothes, French perfumes, lined umbrellas, Beauvais bags, French pepper grinders, Madame de Pompadour dolls—all at prices for more than 30% off.

Suggested gifts from Oberon include French wood and porcelain pepper grinder with salt shaker to match, $9.50; Lalique glass bulls, $17.40; fireproof porcelain sauce pans (with hand-painted flowers on them) $7.00; a shorty nightgown for a new baby, embroidered with rosebuds, $5.00; umbrella with flowered lining and handsome gold carved handle, $14.50; unlined umbrella with reed handle, $7.00; cheese-keeper (water container), $29.50.

The best mail order buy from Paris is perfume. At our local drug store a half ounce of Chanel No. 5 is priced at $15.82 (state and federal taxes included). The same perfume ordered from Paris, comes at a cost of $6.53, for the perfume, $1.00 for postage; 17% duty now based on the retail price, a little more than $1.00. Total price, $8.64. Due to trademark restrictions, the trademark may be obliterated. At that price, do you care? Chanel, without the name, doth smell as sweet.

Begin now to collect catalogues from around the world. Compare local and overseas prices. Keep up with customs regulations (they are constantly changing).

Books, records, art objects, and seeds are the old standbys in mail order. The books that are advertised for mail order, at first glance, are not always bargains in that you cannot buy them below wholesale cost, unless you get a chance to pick up the book you want from a dealer in publishers' overstocks.[4]

Collectors of rare books are the persons who can benefit from ordering by mail. Look in any issue of *Saturday Review*. In the classified section in the back of the weekly magazine you will find ads for French, German, Spanish and Italian books. Many catalogues are offered free. Are the books offered in the catalogues bargains? Often, only in the sense that someone else is doing

---

[4] For any number of reasons a publisher may have "bet wrong" on a book, in which case he may have printed more books than he can sell. He unloads these books to a mail order house, which sells them far below the original book store price.

the searching for you. If you had to take the time to search the world over for an out-of-print book in a foreign language to complete a book of your own or a thesis or a dissertation, you would spend far more. Never discount the time-saving factor in mail order buying.

One of the most interesting catalogues that comes to our house is one published by Norm Flayderman, world authority on antique military equipment, who happens to live right down the road from us on Squash Hollow Road, New Milford, Conn. His catalogue, which you can get for $1.00 a year, is mailed to collectors all over the world and contains news of rare books on the subject of military and seagoing equipment, as well as actual collections.

By far the largest mail order houses for books in the United States are the *Book-of-the-Month Club,* 345 Hudson Street, New York City, and *Literary Guild of America,* 277 Park Avenue, New York City. A recent enrollment offer for the *Book-of-the-Month Club* is a six volume set of books which usually sells for $40, for $1.00 a book. A tremendous savings! And a great library builder! When you enroll, you sign a contract to buy (usually) four books per year. Many of these books are popular books, and you often pay less than the regular retail price. Sometimes, you get 10% off, or 20% off or 30% off on a book. The high priced elegant books offered in the Book-of-the-Month catalogue are the ones with the highest discount. You can see at a glance how Book-of-the-Month comes out on this. (And the *Literary Guild* operates the same way.) By selecting a book as an offer of the month, the club not only helps to popularize a book but offers a publisher a tremendous market. By offering to buy thousands of books, the club gets a discount.

The record clubs pattern their operation after the *Book-of-the-Month Club* program. Both *Columbia Record Club,* Terre Haute, Indiana, and the *RCA Victor Record Club,* which was formerly owned by the *Book-of-the-Month Club,* but is now owned by *Reader's Digest* of Pleasantville, New York, offer come-ons of, maybe 3 records for 97 cents. These three are records that really sell for about $3.98 each. This offer is made on the condition that you become a member of the club. It is an easy way to begin your record library. By figuring that first come-on offer as part of your first year's subscription, you do get 30% off. *New members get the best bargains!*

Seeds, bulbs and trees are sold by mail, but this is nothing new. George Washington ordered his seedlings from England.

Our local nursery imports its bulbs from Holland. This is a strong selling point. But you can do the same and avoid the local markup. Send to J. Heemskerk, c/o P. Van Deursen, Sassenheim, Holland, for a catalogue. Prices of bulbs are reasonable and delivery costs are prepaid.

Look in the garden magazines, the travel magazines, your local newspaper, foreign newspapers. Once again save clippings, order flowers and trees by mail. Your garden can be an exotic place.

In buying books, records, and seeds, look for the introductory or the *reason behind* the price cut. Sometimes, a book serves to promote the organization that sends it out. (*Example:* Good Housekeeping's *Complete Book of Needlecraft* calls attention to Good Housekeeping Magazine every time you open it up. Order it by mail and you get a special subscriber price of $2.00 off the regular price. $5.95 instead of $7.95, its original price.)

McGraw-Hill offers a Color Slide Program of Art Enjoyment. Again it has the "new member" merchandising gimmick. "Accept this album of Italian Renaissance paintings which includes 24 color slides and illustrated 48-page guidebook for only $1 plus a few cents shipping."

"If I continue my subscription," the small print reads, "you will send me a new Color Slide Album every two months (for 10 days trial examination) and bill me at the subscribers' low price of $7.95 plus shipping."

The come-on offer in each case is the real bargain.

Food and beverages

We have already discussed the ordering of liquor by mail from a plane. Many foods and non-alcoholic beverages can be ordered by mail without having to take off in a plane to get the coupon.

Harry & David, Bear Creek Orchards, Medford, Oregon sell pears, plums, superior fruit by mail. So do Hesperian Orchards, Inc., Box 741, Wenatchee, Washington and Pinnacle Orchards, Inc., Box 1068, Medford, Oregon.

Candy from Switzerland is available by mail, and fruit cakes from Virginia, Creole delicacies from New Orleans, but usually when you order foods, you pay for quality and you do not get big price cuts. But you certainly will eat well. Say you love cheese. There's a Cheese-of-the-Month Club with a different kind of cheese coming each month from a different country. Write to Cheese-of-All-Nations, 235 Fulton Street, New York 7, New York for a free catalogue. Or do you live in the midwest and love lobsters? You can order them—*live delivery guaranteed*—eight lobsters (with a first course of steamer clams included) for $23.75, plus express collect, from Saltwater Farms, Inc., Damariscotta 14, Maine.

Miscellaneous

Look for mail order items *everywhere!* In the newspaper today is a Gimbel's ad offering flame red fiberglass curtains that look like burlap, $8.99 a pair, allow three weeks delivery.

In the mail is a catalogue from Edmund Scientific Company, Barrington, New Jersey, offering a pocket sized hand warmer for fishermen for $1.39 postpaid, a "make your own slide" kit for $1.60, an astronomy telescope, 60 to 180 power, $29.95 ppd.

From Altman's we have news of a souffle set, formerly $15, for $12.75. From the Southern New England Telephone Company we have a list of more than 50 educational films which will be sent, free this time, to clubs for programs. "Just send in the card." And from Marjorie Follmer, editor of the *New York City News-letter,* we have an offer for back copies at a savings. The letter is filled with news about small shops, out of the way places, mail order houses where big bargains are available.

We quote from one issue.

Shop of the Month is the *Locate Market,* at 89th Street, 1712 Second Avenue. After hotels and houses have been wrecked, these people buy up usable shutters, chandeliers, mouldings, anything that can be resold. It is surprising how well-designed most of the objects are! The interior of the shop is dusty, but low prices compensate. Hurricane lamps at about $4 apiece may suit your fancy. And you may select a glass lamp globe, an antique, from a large stock in many sizes, shapes and even in different colors. Shutters sell for about $5 per panel. Advice comes free if you need it.

Marjorie writes that she will sell a set of her newspapers about New York City, 18 of them—6 pages each—for $4.00. Mail your check to Marjorie Follmer, N. Y. C. Newsletter, Box 224, Noroton, Connecticut. Her material which she has brought up to date with hand-written notations is specific, well researched and brings news of bargains which you can buy through mail order (or in person if you are planning a trip to New York).

Mail order can save you money, once you get the hang of it, and dress up your life.

8

Find a Charity Bazaar

Rummage sale committee members often get donations of new merchandise. Their husbands may make cigarette cases, or publish books, or be jewelers, bedding manufacturers, or candy makers.

Go to a church bazaar and you will come home with bottles of shampoo at far below the drug store price, cosmetics and good costume jewelry priced at dollar store prices. (At a recent Jewish Bazaar in Massachusetts, new girdles sold for 25 cents a girdle.) Your mood when you go to such a sale should be that "anything might turn up here."

Mary Vogt at the USO office in France, now director of the office in Greece, told us that many well-dressed women in Paris wait for the annual Episcopal Church Bazaar as eagerly as they wait for February Couture Sales. "The parish is a very wealthy one," she told us, "and the dresses members donate are marvelous."

You can get good buys at a church bazaar if the following conditions exist:

1. A few high-priced items are on sale with many low-priced items. If so, the high-priced items will be reduced.

A cosmetics manufacturer may donate 12 or 15 compacts to the bazaar. If they retail at $3 a piece at the local drug store, they will go for $1.98 at the bazaar. Churchwomen will pick them up for gifts.

But at this same Bazaar, there may be a pair of real tortoise-shell spectacle frames on display. The retail price for the frames may be $35 to $45. The marker knows that customers will never pay a high price for used tortoise shell frames, so she will put a tag of $2.50 on them. If they aren't sold until late in the sale, the price will come down to 50 cents. If the frames are flattering to you, have your prescription duplicated in sun glasses and use these frames. A real bargain!

Spectacle cases at such sales which retail for 65 cents to $1 will bring a dime apiece. Now suppose someone donates a fine leather case that was purchased in France for $3? Markers will mark this case at 10 cents too, certainly at no more than 25 cents. Find that case and you get a buy!

2. Are the buyers spending no more than an average of $15 apiece?

At a sale or a store where all items are small, a large item may be a nuisance. Therefore, the salespeople will push it to get it out of the way.

A giant oil painting may be donated. The committee doesn't know what to do with it. One member who knows frames of this size are selling for $80 or $90 at antique shops says, "Oh, I'll give $15 for it if nobody wants it." She goes home with a prize!

3. Do you know quality merchandise when you see it?

If all around you customers are buying poor quality merchandise and you recognize in the midst of it a lovely crystal bowl, pewter candlesticks, or a butter-soft leather bag, you are fortunate. Buyers at a sale of second hand things do not always recognize quality.

You can't take a linen buyer, a crystal collector, a leather expert and other authorities to a church bazaar with you. But if you are attracted to something, a mink collar, for instance, and you do not know whether it has real value, ask the most knowledgeable woman on the committee (the most traveled woman and/or the most exquisitely turned out) to tell you whether the fur is of good quality.

Quick Tests of Quality

1. Is crystal fine?

Ring it! Thump the rim with your fingertip. If the resultant ring is high, the crystal is excellent. The higher the pitch, the more lead in the crystal—a sure test of quality, Tiffany's says.

2. Is the fabric linen or cotton?

Moisten your finger and feel it. Cool? It's linen. Linen absorbs moisture—the fabric *feels* cool because the moisture has been taken from your finger.

3. Lace real or machine made?

Check the back. Any threads or knots or irregularities? It's probably machine-made.

4. Is this really sterling silver?

If it says sterling, it *is* sterling. This is a law. (Only a silver with a minimum amount of alloy, set by the government, can be so marked.)

There will be many other tests of quality, along with a sixth sense which you will develop, which will lead you to quality as others all around you push to buy flashy but less valuable merchandise. They will go home with a painted plaster Dutch boy made in Japan. You will go home with a set of seven (there should be eight, but you can't have everything) beautiful crystal wine glasses. Now you are buying wisely!

9

Look for "Seconds" and "Irregulars"

There *is* a difference between merchandise advertised as "irregular" and merchandise advertised as a "second."

When a white-walled tire is advertised as "irregular" the white on the tire may not be truly circular, a little "off." The manufacturer's name, if it is a big-name manufacturer like Goodyear, Firestone, or U.S. Rubber, is buffed off, and the tire is offered at a reduced price.

When a tire has a true flaw in the rubber (an actual hole which has been plugged up) the tire is advertised as a "second." The name of the manufacturer is again buffed off. The tire is sold as is.

Usually, "irregulars" do not have the price slashed as do the "seconds," because the flaw is slight. (In women's stockings, "seconds" have a snag or a thread inconsistency, while "irregulars" may simply have an irregular hemline at the top or a color band around the top which does not go in a true circle. In the last few years, stores have often used the two terms interchangeably. This is unfortunate because "irregulars" usually will give longer wear than will "seconds.")

Look for "irregulars." Who cares if a white-walled rear tire is slightly less than true? Who cares if one napkin of your madeira luncheon set has three flowers embroidered on it instead of four? Who cares if the lining of a skirt is slightly "off" in colortone from the skirt itself?

Decide whether the irregularity affects performance. If not, buy.

The Purpose

If you are renting a room to someone or furnishing an apartment to rent, look for "irregulars." An "irregular" bed may be structurally perfect, but the veneer may be heavy in one spot on the footboard. An "irregular" vase may have a bubble in the glass. None of these irregularities will affect performance.

Don't consider "seconds" if you want durability. A "second" in a bed may be one with a cracked frame. A replacement will soon be called for. A "second" in a dresser scarf may be one with a hole in the fabric. A "second" in a vase may be one with a crack in it, no good for flowers.

When buying for yourself

Never buy "seconds" in women's stockings unless they are reduced 50%, and never buy unless you buy six pairs at one time—all in the same color. If you come out with four pairs of serviceable stockings, you will be ahead. If the flaws are in the rim or the foot, you may get some wear from all six pairs—and long wear from four matched-up pairs when four flawed stockings have given out.

Never buy "seconds" or "irregulars" without looking for the flaw. If you can't find it, ask the clerk to point it out.

Many kilns, candlemakers, factories and manufacturers have stores on the premises where "seconds" and "irregulars" are sold. If there is a pottery factory near you, or a glass-making factory or a mill, get acquainted with it.

Take a trip through any factory near to you. When you take such a tour, you usually are given a kit of samples. (When you tour the Procter & Gamble factory in Iowa City, Iowa, you not only see what engineers term the finest factory of its kind in the middle west, you will be given a kit of products, not seconds, which includes Crest or Gleam Toothpaste, Secret Deodorant, Liquid Prell Shampoo and often other drug products.)

In touring a mill or pottery factory, you can learn whether there is a factory store on the premises. One sweater factory in Michigan has a room where "seconds" and "irregulars" are sold. For a fraction of the retail cost, you can buy a fine wool sweater or a handsome sweater coat which has a flaw as minor as an undersized buttonhole or a snag in the binding. Several glassmakers in New Jersey sell "seconds." The "seconds" in these factories are fine enough to be purchased as gifts.

Gifts

Give merchandise purchased as "seconds" or "irregulars" as gifts. But select carefully.

We found, for our newly married daughter, a gold-glazed pottery cigarette box at a factory store near a kiln in Pennsylvania, for 70% less than the regular market price. The "second" was an irregular stripe in the stripes of dark and misty gold. If anything, the irregularity adds to its attractiveness.

At Woodstock, New York, we found a candle molded as if it were a night candle in an old-fashioned candle-stick holder. It was a "second" because some of the wax-colored candle had run down on the brown wax "candlestick" base. Scarcely noticeable but worth a 40% reduction. We sent it to a friend as a thank you gift for putting us up one night after a dinner party in their Long Island home. Our hostess was delighted. Only rule we have in buying this kind of merchandise is "no structural flaws." Otherwise, we prefer buying a pair of fine percale pillow slips for 50% *or more* off at a sale of "irregulars" than to buy a pair of muslin pillow slips for the same price.

10

Join a Consumer Organization

Send a post card to the following asking for full information about each:

1. *Consumers Digest*
   6316 N. Lincoln Avenue
   Dept. 85
   Chicago, Illinois

2. *Consumers Union of the United States, Inc.*
   256 Washington Street
   Mount Vernon, New York

The cost of becoming a member of Consumers Digest, according to our latest records, is $7.00 per year. Membership entitles you to the following:

1. Six issues per year of *Consumers Digest Magazine.*
   Here are some of the typical subjects: Money-Saving Tips on Income Tax; Your Children Can Study Abroad; Product Reports on Electric Knives, Shavers, Toasters, Encyclopedias; Maximum Life Insurance Protection at Lowest Cost; Discount Prices on Diamonds; The Two Year College.

2. *Consumers Digest's* Annual Price-Buying Directory.
   The Directory tells you what *the dealer* has had to pay for a particular model of dishwasher, tape recorder, automobile or anything else you are buying.
   (Here are steps you are advised to take when buying an

automobile: (1) determine what car you want; (2) write down what the dealer paid for it (the price is in the Directory); (3) check the standard equipment listing to see what is included with the auto; (4) determine what accessories you want (check the Directory for these costs); (5) determine freight charges of the auto by looking on the windshield; (6) total all the costs, auto, freight and accessories. You now have the complete dealer cost including federal taxes. (7) Now add a minimum profit of $100-$125 for a Chevy, Ford, Falcon, Oldsmobile, Valiant; $125-$150 for a Buick, Pontiac, Rambler; $150-$175 for a Mercury; $200-$225 for a T-bird; $500 for a Lincoln Continental; $550-$750 for a Cadillac. Such homework leads to better buying.)

3. A membership card which entitles you to buy for a specific discount price (often as much as 30% off) from Directory dealers.

4. A library card which lets you write for answers about buying anything.

These services make up the $7.00 per year membership fee many times over.

Consumers Union

Consumers Union is a testing organization which sends out monthly reports, paid for by members, who pay an annual fee of $6.00. The source of CU's income is the sale of its publications to members, subscribers and newsstand buyers. In one report last year's income was $4,000,000.

Each December the Union publishes "*Consumer Reports*", ($1.75). The book is divided into sections such as: *Yourself; Your Home; Your Household; Your Leisure.* Under *Yourself,* the Guide reports on everything from bras to sunglasses, from men's shirts to electric toothbrushes. Brands are named—tests are explained in full. In the *Your Leisure* section, tests of cameras, sleds,

TV antennas are reported. Consumers Union is a testing organization which brings you reports of everything from high protein cereals to binoculars. *Consumers Digest* is a price guide to discount buying. Both services can help you become a better purchasing agent.

11

Shop the Classifieds

We have two classified directories. One is the 134 page classified section in the digest-sized Litchfield County telephone book. The second is the New York City Red Book with 1,956 large yellow pages.

In New Milford and New York City we shop the yellow pages. We save on gas this way in the country, and on bus and taxi fares in the city.

Unlimited calls is part of our telephone service in the country. So when we want a *carpenter,* we call several before driving all over Litchfield County to find what different carpenters charge for specific jobs. And we call several seamstresses for charges when we want slipcovers made. Comparison shopping by telephone makes good sense in the country.

In New York, we are charged per telephone call. Message units mount up. To call six columns of carpenters is ridiculous. We still shop the classifieds, but we limit our calls to places three or four blocks from the apartment. We conclude each transaction in person, but by telephoning in advance we save time and frustration.

Use the telephone for shopping in all these cases:

1. *When you are information hunting about prices or services.*

2. *When a bargain is offered by a store to attract shoppers.*
   Avoid crowds—order by phone unless a "No telephone order" is advertised or unless examination is necessary.

(*Example:* You may want some golf clubs for your young son. You see "Sam Snead Young Champ—complete sets—advertised for $39.00. You believe this is a good buy for a driver, spoon, 3, 5, 7, 9 irons, putter and bag. You check Consumers Digest's *Guide to Consumer Buying,* find that the list price for this set is $65.50, the purchase price offered to Consumers Digest members, $42.89. You look back at the ad—$39 for the complete set. A come on! You can get a spectacular bargain. Ordering by telephone makes sense.)

3. *When you are in a hurry and time means money.*
   If you live in a large city, maintain one charge account at a good grocery store, even though you may do most of your shopping at a supermarket. Keep an *emergency menu* glued in the bottom of a kitchen drawer. When unexpected guests descend, call your grocer and order emergency rations. You will save money and time if you substitute a telephone order for frantic rushing.

FOLLOW THESE SIMPLE RULES FOR EFFICIENT TELEPHONE BUYING:

1. Know exactly what service you want from a carpenter, a seamstress, or anyone else before you ask for a price.

2. Call with the ad in front of you if you are ordering an advertised product.

3. Order from a list when you order groceries. Ask for prices if your grocer makes suggestions.

4. Write down a list of five appointment times *convenient to you* before you call a doctor, a dentist, a barber or beauty shop.

5. When you call for information about something like wallpaper and plan to make your final selection in person, ask to have the merchandise ready for inspection when you get to the shop.

6. Get the name of the person to whom you are talking. A little foresight when shopping by telephone makes for better buying.

12

Watch for "Special Days"

Stores have many reasons to cut prices every month. Learn the six basic reasons behind the price dips, and you will get some fortunate buys.

The sensible six

Here are the reasons merchants cut prices.

1. To flag customers with come-on merchandise to increase store traffic.
2. To avoid spoilage in food.
3. To get rid of seasonally dead merchandise.
4. To clear the floor for new merchandise.
5. To get rid of imperfect merchandise.
6. To get rid of "lemons" or duds.

In the mail box today is an Anniversary Sale announcement from a store in Danbury. "Tube type or tubeless tires—no trade-in required—your choice $5.99." And from New York comes a department store headliner, "Reconditioned typewriters—$78; after sale, $99.50." And from the local hardware store, "100 pruning shears, $1.27 each, regular price $3.50. *Come while supply lasts.*"

If you can go into a store, pick up the headliner, and then come home, you can get exceptional bargains. Leaders often make the merchant no profit. His profit comes from the other things you buy.

Follow these rules when buying bargain foods.

1. Don't buy if the taste is affected, do buy if just the appearance is changed. A clever cook can make almost any food look good.

2. Don't buy fruit and green things with bad spots. When these spots are cut away, you have no bargain.

3. Do buy day old bread for toast. (The price is always down.)

4. Do buy bananas with brown specks; they're better this way.

5. Do buy melted chocolate bars (and chocolate Easter Eggs the day after Easter). Freeze and slice them.

The week after Christmas, Christmas cards are "dead." Christmas candy is marked down and the grocery store which has overstocked on dates marks them down.

Evening gowns are marked down after the town's big holiday dance. Live Easter bunnies can be bought for half price or more the day after Easter.

If you have a need for merchandise after a holiday, you are in luck. (Example: You may be moving south when bathing suits are being packed away up north. Get your suit at an end-of-season sale. Don't wait till you get to where suits are in demand.)

Watch the local store that advertises a huge sale of heavy hardware, like outdoor tables. Unless that store has plenty of storage space, left over tables will be sold at the end of summer to make ready for fireplace tools and wood boxes. Buy your outdoor table then. Seasonally dead merchandise costs far less.

Less-than-perfect merchandise

Irregulars and seconds are automatically marked down. Merchandise soiled from too much handling is marked down later. Merchandise which has been tried on too often (or has a tear) hits the final mark-down rack.

Baby clothes at a recent church sale were snatched up at 75 cents a dress. These were lovely dresses with tiny hand-made button holes, beautifully embroidered. But they were soiled, so they were donated by an exclusive baby shop. One sophisticated woman told me that she laundered, pressed, and stuffed each little dress with pink tissue paper, gave to new mothers.

The buyers at the sale at Christ Church on Park Avenue were better buyers than were the customers at the baby shop.

Look in shops at the mark-down counter. Less-than-perfect merchandise often can be made perfect again and can be bought for very little. The 75 cent baby dresses sold at the church originally were sold for $11.

Slack season prices

In small towns in the winter time, house painters, carpenters, and contractors are not busy. If you can have your house papered (or even built) *then* rather than in the summer, you will save money. Women who give permanent waves, secretaries who are hired only during a contractor's busy summer rush, and men who work in boat yards want extra work in the winter. Get help then.

What bargains to look for when

Here are 12 times during the year when merchandise can be bought for far less right in your own home town.

1. *During the 2 weeks after Christmas:* Buy fruit cakes, dates, candied fruits, Christmas candy, Christmas ornaments (especially slightly damaged ones such as glass balls with the loops torn out), Christmas and New Year's cards (especially those not wrapped in packages), Christmas wrappings. Get ballgowns in specialty shops, evening wraps, obvious Christmas presents like lamé blouses, bracelet and earring sets, compacts, evening bags.

2. *January:* Buy furs. (Better to buy now than in August. August sales are a merchandising gimmick; January sales are real mark-downs. Furriers have to get rid of furs rather than pay for storage next summer.) Winter clothes (the buyers are

getting ready for spring, want to unload). Get the *come-ons* at White Sales. The January White Sale is a merchandising gimmick, but the come-ons (on enormous bath towels or seconds in pillow slips or last year's big color like purple or orange) can be real buys.

3. *At the end of February:* Get Valentine and George Washington party favors, snow suits, sleds, overcoats.

4. *In March:* Buy inexpensive skis and outdoor toys, stereo equipment, TV sets.

5. *In April:* Get hats at after-Easter sales, and other women's things.

6. *In May:* Buy come-ons at sales of camping and boating equipment, garden tools.

7. *In June:* Buy seasonally dead winter and early spring clothes for both women and men.

8. *In July:* Take advantage of off-season specials at winter resorts. (Buy through a travel agent.) Go to final sales of spring clothes.

9. *In August:* Buy summer clothes—(stores have to clear out for winter clothes).

10. *In September:* Buy automobiles. (The new cars will soon be out, and your dealer wants to get rid of left-over cars from last year's purchase.) Also, get bargains on canned and frozen foods. The new "pack" has now been processed. Food processed from last year's crop, if this year's crop is a big one, will be marked down.

11. *In October:* Buy boats, summer camp merchandise, lawn furniture. (All merchandise that is difficult to store during the winter is reduced if it is not sold.)

12. *In November:* This is the month to buy a house. (Most home owners have about given up selling a house which has been listed all summer. By December, these same owners will decide that the house can be sold in the spring.)

Do It Yourself

Not long ago we put a fieldstone fireplace into one end of our kitchen. We were lucky to find blasted granite for facing on our property. We hired a man, got a truck, went up into the field and collected the granite pieces. We knew exactly how we wanted the fireplace to look, knew where the chimney was to be placed, and where we wanted to build into it an outdoor grill. We made the plans. We furnished the stone. We bought the sand and cement to be mixed into mortar and the firebrick for the lining. (Total cost of collecting materials—$150.)

Now we had to hire a skilled mason and his helper. (The mason always works with a helper, who mixes the mortar and carries it to his boss.) To get a mason we had to go through a cost-plus contractor who added 10% to our bill. By the time we had our fireplace we had paid $1800 for labor plus 10% (or $180) more to the contractor who got the skilled workman and his helper for us. Not long after this the mason built an exact copy of this fireplace for his own house. By doing the work himself, he saved almost $2,000 in labor costs.

You save far more than 30% when you do work for yourself rather than hire someone, but to do this you (1) have to be skilled in some line, and (2) have to have the intelligence to begin with a good idea.

If you have the skill to do, as well as the creative ability to see, you can save thousands of dollars a year. Without the creative ability, you can still save thousands by borrowing from others.

You can get a pattern if you sew, a plan for a building if you build, a plan for clearing the land, if you have land to clear. Such services are provided by magazines, the government, individuals. Or you can adapt ideas. The skilled seamstress who can adapt a design for a Paris suit will be well dressed; the home gardener who can lay out beds after a plan conceived by a landscape gardener for a nearby estate will have beautiful grounds; the home craftsman who can adapt a design for a beautiful piece of furniture will have an interesting home.

Pictured in our newspaper today is a chest designed by Jules Risom (77 inches long by 20 inches wide) which contains six file cabinets. It stands on four short sturdy legs, contains all the filing space any efficient home will ever need. (Exterior is black walnut with a natural oil finish, pulls for the file cabinet are aluminum with black anodized finish.) Cost is $780.

Here you are paying for *the idea*. A carpenter assures us he can duplicate the chest for less than $150. The trick is to find a good idea, then, adapt it.

Many service magazines provide "handyman" ideas to readers. *Better Homes and Gardens* recently ran a story about a desk with space for a typewriter, two single drawer file cabinets, plus drawer and pigeonhole space.

The plan for making this space-saver (3403-A 3) out of a plywood box, can be ordered from Better Homes and Gardens, Des Moines, Iowa, for $2.00. Diagrams show you how to fit the pieces.

Unpainted furniture vs. painted furniture

Macy's occasionally runs an ad featuring a piece of painted furniture for one price; unpainted for at least 30% less. The Sears store in Danbury gave us prices of painted and unpainted furniture. A chest of 10 drawers, unpainted is $30. The same chest painted (which in this case Sears does not carry) would be $45. You are paying that extra 33⅓% for the paint plus the labor.

Buying unpainted furniture is a wise way to buy, if you buy realistically. The $30 chest at Sears is unpainted pine, sturdy enough for a baby's room or for extra storage space. Anyone should be able to paint this chest. But if you can't paint, buy the unpainted version anyway, and the paint (approximately $1.14 for the undercoat, $1.49 for the overcoat). Get a handyman to do the painting in an hour for $3.00 tops. Even by hiring the painting done, you save about $10.

One of our daughter's husbands argues that if he is going to pay $30 for a chest, he prefers to spend that sum at an auction, a second hand place or a Salvation Army store. He says he will have a much handsomer chest in the long run.

The unpainted-painted display of two objects is a merchandising trick, to get you to buy the unpainted one. You may be able to get a more beautiful piece of furniture someplace else for *the same price*. (It may be chipped or scarred or broken but it will be elegant when refinished, which the pine chest can never be.)

Your city may have a showroom outlet (New York has one at 229 West 64th Street) where you can buy worn wares at wholesale (or lower) prices. Maxine and Clayton Donahue, owners of the New York store, collect samples from showrooms when their showcase days are over. (Such merchandise used to be shipped back and burned at factories or sold for scrap.) In the Donahues' showroom, Knoll, Raynor, Ficks Reed and other manufacturers' and importers' designs (mostly modern) are offered at slashed prices. Recently, a Knoll's flower-shaped coffee table that lists for $210 sold for $125, a Ficks Reed dining room table that ordinarily sells for $255 sold for $125 and matching chairs were marked down from $97.80 to $50. A hutch was marked down from $150 to $90. Light fixtures which retailed for $60 went down to $40.

If anyone wants a top from one table and a base from another at Showroom Outlets, he can get this. If he wants a piece of furniture refinished (there goes the price up, however) he can have this done. No delivery is made (the customer arranges for that) and no returns are accepted.

Suppose you find a chest here that has been scarred or scratched in a showroom? The price will be higher, scratch and all, than you will pay for an unpainted piece of furniture, but once you do a refinishing job at home, you will have a much better piece of furniture than you will have when you paint the unpainted furniture. If you like the best in modern furniture, find discards from showrooms. If you like antiques, go to an auction. Do the refinishing or painting yourself.

Can you sew?

One billion dollars was spent last year by American women on fabric, patterns, sewing machines, notions and thread, more than ever before in American history. Even the teen-agers have gone in for sewing. The New York *Times* reports that 22,500,000 garments were made by high school girls last year, and adds, "they made shifts by the bushel basket." One hundred million patterns are sold every year by Vogue, the McCall Corporation, Simplicity Pattern Company, Butterick, and Advance.

If you learn to sew even a little bit, you can make some of your clothes. (Pattern-makers are simplifying patterns every year.) And if you can sew well, you can have couture fashions. The Vogue designer-pattern series now comprises some 50 styles by 18 designers like Gres, Marc Bohan of Dior, Simonetta and others. The patterns cost $2 to $3.50. Other patterns by other houses not specializing in couture clothes run about 50 cents for a blouse pattern, 65 to 75 cents for a dress pattern and $1 to $1.50 for a suit. You can make a wool suit that would retail at $40 or $50 for $8 or $10.

Singer offers eight sewing lessons for $12.50, when you buy a machine. (Regular price for these lessons, $25.) The company runs an annual sewing contest for girls between 10 and 21 (first prize—a trip to Paris) and publishes a series of 25 cent booklets, each devoted to a specific sewing problem. Typical title: *"Holiday Gifts to the Sewhandy."*

Machines, fabrics, and fashions are constantly changing for the better. No wonder millions are making shifts, sleeveless jumper dresses (a runaway best seller) and *pillows* (*McCall's all-time best seller*). Are you? This is a foolproof money saver.

Buy in Quantity

"People come in and buy a couple of pork chops or a small piece of steak, and they think they're not spending much," our butcher told us. "At the end of the month their meat bill is twice as high as it should be!"

Study these simple mathematics: One 14 pound ham at a local store costs 79 cents a pound, or $11.06. One center slice of this same ham (cut ½ to ¼ inch thick) costs $1.35 a pound. One 14 pound ham will give you 10 to 12 slices (not all center cuts, of course) which average about 84 cents a pound. You save 40% when you buy in quantity.

Here's why the butcher sells for less when he sells in quantity.

1. He spends as little time making a large sale as he does in making a small one.

2. He clears out space, and storage space is worth money.

3. He saves himself the work of dividing and merchandising small items.

Buy in quantity and you save the merchant *money*. Ask for a discount when you buy this way from a meat man, a grocer, or fruit man.

At a farmer's stand the other night we saw small yellow tomatoes for sale at 25¢ per half pint. The farmer had eight boxes left. It was late. He would have more fresh tomatoes to sell in the morning. "We'll take all eight for $1.35," we said. The farmer was glad to close up the stand.

When our six small grandchildren come we buy jars of baby food by the case and get 8% or more off the regular price. We recently picked up 10 cases from our grocer's warehouse. The grocer didn't have to stack the cans on the shelves; he didn't have to sell by the can; he had cash on the line. Also, he didn't have to deliver the merchandise. We asked for a discount and got it. (This grocer is a friend of ours. All won't bother.)

Save on clothes by buying quantity. Today, we have a brochure from Grant's Store. Two pair of Sanforized undershorts, $1.—is what one ad reads. *Save $1.14 on 6 pairs.* $3.00 for six—instead of the usual $4.14 bought one at a time. About a third off.

Buy paint by the quart and you pay more than you do when you buy by the gallon. From an ad today: Paint, $1.30 per quart— $4.35 per gallon—(you save 85 cents.) The more you buy, the more you save.

Sometimes, a merchant limits a quantity purchase bargain to "so many to a customer." For instance, from Grant's folder we see "package of 10 Cannon terry washcloths, regular $1.00, now 84 cents." *Limit, 2 packages per customer.* When you see one like this, *buy*. The offer is a come-on to get you to buy other things in the store. You save 32 cents on a regular $2.00 purchase. Save 30% by taking the discount on several different come-on items. Ten men's handkerchiefs—74 cents, limit, *1 set* per customer. You save 26 cents here. So now you are saving 58 cents on a $3.00 purchase. And here's another: "Wearever Pen with 12 ink cartridges, 67 cents, regularly $1.00. Limit 1 per customer." Now you are saving 91 cents on $4.00. About 25% off for all your purchases, and if you buy one more "Limit, one to a customer" item you will save 30%.

Merchants often offer something other than a price cut when you buy in quantity. Abraham & Strauss offers to sew name tapes in free when you buy camp clothing (for children going away to camp) in an order of $25 or more. B. Altman does the same thing in New York. Gimbels stencils the child's name and address on his or her trunk and ships the trunk free if the child's parents order $10 or more of supplies.

In New York, on the Avenue of the Americas, between 25th and 26th streets, and also on East Houston Street, there are flea markets patterned after the one in Paris. Litchfield, Connecticut, has an annual May-day flea market. There may be a flea market near you. At a market like this, bargain when you buy in quantity. Once at the Houston Street flea market we saw a display of buttons and eagles from old-time U. S. Army uniforms. They were spread out on the flat hood of a station wagon—and priced from 25 cents to $1.00 apiece. We bought all the stock for $7.00. What did we use them for? For buttons on a Chanel-type at-home jacket (with matching pants). We had an eagle soldered on a bracelet (stunning!); we had a scarf clip made out of one eagle (the delight of one who got it for Christmas).

Buy 12 pairs of stockings, get one pair free. Not 30% off—but if you shop until you find stockings of a good brand sale-priced at something like "3 for $2.55" you can save 30% by the time you buy your 12 pairs.

Several years ago a South American workman found one of the world's largest diamonds in a river. He sold it to a man who sold it again, and this man sold it once more; and it was sold even again. Eventually, a wealthy American bought the diamond for $235,000. He cut up the massive diamond, and sold off the pieces. He made exactly one million dollars. Little pieces of something go for more. Buy in quantity.

15

Work It Out —
Or Trade It In!

In gathering material for this book, we wrote to the heads of the state development commissions in the 50 states. We asked each one for the names of places in the state where individuals can do work in exchange for merchandise. (*Example: Cut down five Christmas trees for a grower, get one free.*)

Our letter from New Hampshire contains the following information about things that can be bought for less there if you do the picking, cutting or other work:

Pick-your-own apples, $1 per bushel, against $2.50 when already picked.

Pick-your-own blueberries, 15 cents against 40 to 50 cents.

Pick-your-own strawberries, 20 to 25 cents against 50 to 60 cents.

Cut-your-own Christmas tree, $2.00 as against $3.00 in the marketplace downtown.

There are places in Vermont, we are told, where you can take your own jug to a farmer and fill it with maple sap right from the tree. Take it home and boil it down, and you still pay only about half what you pay for syrup sold along the road.

In our letter from South Dakota's Ron Struwe, we got this piece of information. "If you are interested in gold you can make this a do-it-yourself project in South Dakota. Mountain streams in the Black Hills are wide open to anyone who wants to pan for gold.[1] Of course, it's a slow and low-paying process."

The absentee owner of a farm in Iowa or in Ohio as in many other midwestern states will pay another farmer to run his farm. In exchange for running it, the man who lives on the farm gets his living plus a share of the profits.

Land owners in many parts of the country will let you hunt on their land if you give them a share of your game. The man with a stocked pond will let you fish in exchange for part of your catch. (When the Conservation Commission stocks a pond, they ask that the pond be fished. You provide a service by fishing.)

In order to find what trades are available to you in your state, write to your State Development Commission, State Capitol Building, and ask for information available to consumers who want to do better buying of state products.

Most commissions publish a directory of all manufacturers in the state. (Some states charge for this. Mississippi charges $5.00 for its book.)

The most complete book we received was sent to us from Minnesota. There, all industries are listed for every town in the state, with each town's specialty described in full. In reading it, we found ourselves wondering if residents near Faribault, the world's peony capital, can pick their own peonies for a reduced price. Can a fisherman make a deal to fish for trout in another man's spring fed lake? Can a man get granite for a fireplace or patio direct from the quarry at St. Cloud? If a hunter at Wheaton shoots ducks on another man's property, does he give in exchange a share of the hunt? Can a man make an arrangement to dig his own peat from the fields near Chisholm? Only by knowing your state can you possibly know what trades may be available to you.

-----

[1] This could be a good vacation for boys, but for the real prospector, grubstaking in Canada will probably be more profitable. There, near where Texas Gulf Sulphur made its strike, you can seek for gold or look for mineral deposits in other parts of Canada in exchange for a share of your discoveries. As a start, send to Director, Geological Survey of Canada, Ottawa, Canada for free booklet "Brief Information on Prospecting for Uranium in Canada" which contains information on prospecting in general.

Trades in your own neighborhood

If there is a pond or swimming pool in your neighborhood, ask its owners if you can teach their children to swim in exchange for your being able to swim there. If someone on your road has lots of lilacs, ask if you can pick some in exchange for baking two pies for these people. The owners of the lilacs will probably tell you to take the flowers and forget the pies. Don't do this. Send the pies. Next year, the owners will be glad to see you come around for more lilacs. Arrange to drive three of your neighbor's children to school which is near where you drive to work or for groceries. Suggest that each of the mothers provide two hours of child care a week for you in exchange for the transportation.

Here are other suggestions for trades.

1. You are a woman living alone. Offer to let an older woman live with you for one month each year as a service to her family. (Not a bedridden woman.) In exchange for providing this change for a grandmother, let the family send you to their summer place when they aren't using it.

2. Let a farm family child who wants to finish a year of school stay in your home. Or provide a room for a handicapped school child. Go to the principal of the school if you are interested.

3. Swap your home and have a free vacation through Vacation Exchange Club which we will discuss later.

4. Provide a *professional* service. (Are you a book reviewer? You will automatically be sent every new book that comes out from every enterprising publisher. Are you a movie critic? You get a pass to any movie you want to see.) When you talk about a new job, think of these on-the-side benefits.

5. Do you have *ideas* for merchandising? An artist can trade design ideas with a local fabric manufacturer. In exchange for a promotional idea—he can get fabrics for draperies for his home.

6. Do you have a stone building on your property? (We know a man who provides one for a man who runs a small creamery. No rent is exchanged. But the lessee provides the lessor with all the cottage cheese, milk, cream, butter, and cream cheese his family eats in a year.)

7. Do you need household help? We hired a woman several years ago to care for *two* of our young children. She came for room and board, and some spending money for *her and her child*. It was great for her, for us and for *all* the children.

8. Want to live at a resort? Decide where. The Virgin Islands? Atlantic City? The Gulf of Mexico? Cape Cod? Select a section of the country where there are many resorts, then apply for work months in advance to every single resort in that part of the country.

9. Do you have a snow plow? We have a friend with a plow who lives on a street which has three homes on it. One woman lives alone on the road. She cannot plow. So our friend keeps the road clear in exchange for the woman's doing babysitting. To make this trade, he said to the woman, "I have an idea. I will keep the road and your driveway clean all winter if you will give us 10 hours a month of baby-sitting for December, January, February and March." She could figure, "At $1.50 an hour for 10 hours a month, I am giving them $15 a month. In exchange they are giving me what I would have to pay an outsider at least $60 a year to do."

Thought to remember when trading: *Suggest a specific trade if you want to make a good deal!*

16

Skip the Doo-Dads!

When we asked a local bakery, "What is the cost of your most popular wedding cake?" the answer was "$29.95, including ornaments."

A 1 pound cake made with the same batter costs $1.50. Sixteen 1 pound cakes cost $24. Yet, the 16 pound wedding cake costs $5.95 more. *Because of the ornaments.*

A new Ford Mustang, purchased with standard equipment, including a heater, costs $2368 in Detroit. Freight to Connecticut adds $75. (Freight to points farther away adds more.) That same car, with frills (radio, clock, power steering, power brakes, special upholstery, including fancy lights) costs $3400 plus freight. The dealer's mark-up on a car is 25%, but his mark-up on accessories is 40%. You will need sales resistance to save 30% here.

Some things are better without the doo-dads

In the case of women's clothes, doo-dads are a *cover-up*. When you see a pin on a dress or a flower or a fancy (not a really good leather) belt, *beware.*

When you buy a car or a house, you will need will-power to forego frills, for two reasons:

1. When you buy a house, a car, or a color TV, you are in the mood to spend money. (The salesman knows this so he pushes accessories.) Be careful, until you get over this "let it rip" mood.

2. Frills lend glamor. It takes courage to look beneath this. What you want is good basic design.

An assistant to Hollywood producer Martin Ransohoff was heard recently to say into a phone "Listen, honey, Marty wants to know if you've got a Jackie Kennedy-type dress for the fudge scene—good God, no! No ruffles." Mrs. Kennedy has done more to improve the taste of American women than has any other feminine figure in the past 200 years. And certainly *she* skips the doo-dads.

Merchandising ideas are doo-dads!

Don't pay for merchandising gimmicks! Let's say you like pine soap and pine scented bath oil. Don't buy them in a box together. Buy your soap and oil separately, and save as much as 30%, sometimes more.

When buying food, get good basics—the best meat, fruit, dairy products, and vegetables that you can buy. Then plan your frills carefully. (Example: If you like the taste of anchovies with almonds, get anchovies at one sale, almonds at another.)

Merchandising men lurk in the laundry with bleaches, detergents, softeners, whiteners. They know that American women *overuse* all, so they get you to buy box after box. Read the labels. Don't add bleach if your detergent has bleach in it. Don't use a water softener or fabric softener if it contains softeners. Work out a washday recipe that is right for your clothes. Then, stick to it.

When buying a house, don't pay for *any* frills. Get land if you can. (Remember in your lifetime there will be a population explosion!) Get good basic construction, a good heating system, a good roof. A fireplace and a second bathroom add to value. (They are not frills!)

Doo-dads send the price up. Don't pay for them. Pay for good basic construction.

17

Publicize Your Needs!

Others approach *you* with merchandising gimmicks every day! How about your merchandising your own services or wares? The easiest way to get what you want is to spread the word.

The last time we went to the dentist, a woman reading a newspaper in the reception room looked up and said, "You don't happen to know anyone around here who has an unusual furnished apartment to rent, do you?" We did happen to know a musician who had a studio to rent. We gave the woman his number, and she left happily on her way to call him. We were not surprised to learn they "connected." She was telling the world exactly what she wanted.

If you adopt the methods of great merchandisers like the Procter & Gamble Company, the Ford Motor Company, the Johnson Wax Company, and others, you will use one or more of the following methods to tell those around you about what you want to sell (or to buy):

1. Advertising
2. Publicity
3. Public Relations

One of our sons recently graduated from the University of Miami in Florida. After every Christmas in his four years there he drove someone north in exchange for the trip up. Year after year, he made the plan work.

He uses all of the three techniques.

He placed a small ad in the school paper and in the local Miami paper which read something like this: WILL DRIVE YOU AND/OR YOUR CAR TO NEW YORK IN EXCHANGE FOR TRIP UP. *Tom Kinney, Tel. no.*

One year he encouraged the editor of the university paper to run a list of students looking for rides and car owners looking for students to share the driving, a good publicity angle.

He told all his friends to tell *their* friends what he had in mind, should the occasion come up. This is a public relations approach. He began his "campaign" right after Thanksgiving, never missed accomplishing his purpose. One Christmas a local business man asked him to drive his car up. The man wanted his car in the north, but didn't want to drive up. He flew. Tom drove.

Today, there is an ad in a New York paper in the *Wanted to Purchase* column, "WANTED SECOND-HAND HARP. No. 17, 19 or 23 in., good condition. Box #___, Times." What do you bet that person has a harp by the end of this week? Here's another. "WANTED FOR CASH. Late model NCR Bkkpg Mach Model 33-17 Totals or 33-21 Totals, Box #___, Times." Another good specific request.

When you want something, anything, a cook or a baby sitter or a ride to the coast (either coast) or a pet or an apartment or a summer place or a mink stole or a used car or *anything* else, put a small ad in the classified section. And be absolutely specific. Specify in your ad *exactly* what you want. Then, wait for the phone to ring or the mail to come in. (Reminder: You will get less write-ins than you will telephone calls.)

How to get what you want

Write down on a piece of paper something *you* want. And once again, be specific.

Write down the steps that will lead to your realization of this want.

If this is something that must come from others, once they know you want it, advertise or use publicity or public relations.

If it is a project (like getting the town to pave your road) make up a plan, facing all obstacles; then, let others help you get what you want. *Spread the word.*

18

Get into a Pool

A cooperative is an association of individuals which has banded together for the purpose of doing business at reduced costs. In a *true* consumer cooperative, a group of consumers set up their own stores. *Surplus* savings (not called profits) at the end of the year are passed back to consumers in proportion to what each has bought at the store.

We do not suggest that you and your friends set up a true cooperative buying group, complete with stores. Although, we do suggest that if you have a retail store near you *run by a co-operative group* that you check prices there. We have an Agway Store near us, which is an outgrowth of Eastern States Cooperative, a farmers' group which has been buying farm machinery, bulbs, seed, lime, and everything else a farmer needs for the past 50 years. We get good farm merchandise here at a good price. (Typical bargain—trash burner regularly $3.95, now $2.99.)

Business men who cannot buy in large quantities, as can cooperative stores, resent the fact that federal legislation has exempted the patronage dividends of cooperatives from corporate income taxes. We are not going to get into the pro and con political implications of large-scale cooperative buying. We simply say that by pooling resources any group of consumers can get things for less.

Lesson to be learned from cooperatives: When you pool your money with other consumers, buy in quantity, then divvy up, you pay less per purchase than when you buy alone.

Consumers often form groups to buy stocks. These consumers form a corporation which is beneficial to their interests in three ways: (1) a decision can be made without all members being present; (2) some tax benefits result from a corporation's being formed, although this is a complicated set-up which varies with cases, so consult your lawyer before making this step yourself; (3) a corporation can purchase stocks in its own name and pay one broker's commission.

Without forming a corporation, there are three advantages to buying stocks with others: (1) in a group one member can research one stock, another can look into another type of stock, etc.; (2) the corporation can buy more shares because more members have more money than does one person; and (3) because of increased funds, diversification is possible.

Some groups spend their profits for a glamorous party. Others give to charity. Others give back the money to members such as a cooperative store gives patronage dividends.

A group of engineers interested in flood control, soil conservation, erosion prevention, etc., are buying land in the New England states. Their aim is to improve the land, develop it, then sell it in lots.

Clubs charter planes for vacation trips—making a good deal on the plane fare, then paying less per person than on a regular flight. We once took a trip to Trinidad on the Ocean Monarch. Once on board we found that the ship had been chartered by the Shrine from Harrisburg, Pennsylvania. The organization agreed to take 200 or 250 tickets for a reduced price. Each person got a better buy than he would have had he bought directly from the liner. (Some places were unfilled at the last minute when we contracted to go.) We paid more than the Harrisburg people, but the ship went all out in entertaining the group and we found ourselves having a marvelous time.

Women have car pools for taking children to school just as men have car pools for going to work, but we know no group of families pooling funds to buy basics. The first group that does this will save money. Just as the price of ham comes down when you buy in quantity rather than by the slice, diapers bought by the gross are less expensive than diapers bought by the dozen; so are sheets and dishtowels and everything else.

Pool your resources with others, whether you are buying land, stocks, groceries, even a ticket at the races. A recent winner of the Daily Double at Roosevelt Raceway won $172,726. He owed the government $101,568 until he produced two partners. Because there were three ticket owners they will only pay a total of $70,500 in taxes, $30,000 less! Reason: the winnings would have put *one* winner into the 80% income bracket. When divided, each winner paid less of a percentage.

19

Bargain!

Here are five don'ts to keep in mind when bargaining:

1. *Don't try to bargain at a chain store.*
   The store has its prices set at the central office.

2. *Don't try to bargain with a clerk in a privately owned store.*
   Only the owner or a strong head of a department is a decision-
   maker.

3. *Don't try to cut the price of merchandise that has a set price
   in all stores.* These "fair trade" items have prices set at the
   manufacturer's home office. Store owners who fiddle with
   these prices can lose their franchise.

4. *Don't pretend to be an expert* when buying from someone who
   knows more about the merchandise than you do.

5. *Don't knock the merchandise!*

Trying to get the price down by any of these methods gets you
nowhere.

Whether you are out to buy a leather pepper grinder on the
Ponte Vecchio in Florence, or a new checked suit for your young
son in Boston, talk price to someone who is in business to make a
profit, not someone who is in the store to wait on customers. *There
is a great difference in the two points of view!*

Some prices are the same everywhere. A food processor or
cosmetic manufacturer or clothing company may supply many

outlets, some located not far from one another. Don't try to get lower than the recommended list price. Discounting below this price can result in a store's loss of permission to sell.

It will be a temptation when bargaining to pretend to be an expert. *Don't.* Do you think the gem merchant won't know whether you really know diamonds? Pretend to know them in a strange market and you may come home with fake stones! Take an expert along, and you will come home with a bargain!

We recently watched a sophisticated European make an irretrievable mistake when trying to get the price down on a house owned by a Connecticut Yankee. He knocked it. "This is a gyp," he said. The owner stiffened, refused to budge in his price. The European could not find a way to pay the asking price and still save face. A week later the Yankee sold for far less than his asking price to someone who liked the house. Don't knock the merchandise!

Now here are three *do's:*

1. *Do* leave your timidity at home! Bargaining is not for the bashful.

2. *Do* know when to bargain and when to forget about it.

3. *Do* be sure the price you offer is right.

Speak up

Many persons are afraid to bargain, believing it will be frowned upon by the seller. The opposite is often the case. A newspaper correspondent in India recalls an experience when he accompanied the first organized American tour party to the Himalayan kingdom of Nepal.

The group admired a collection of temple horns shown to them by the famous China Lama, a "living Buddha" who presides at the great Bodnath Pagoda near Katmandu. Many of the visitors were anxious to own such a horn, but felt that it would be improper to try to buy one from the Lama.

Finally, the holy man said, "If anyone would like to buy a horn, they are 50 rupees."

Moral: *Don't be bashful.*

These people expect you to dicker

1. Merchants catering to tourists.

2. Real estate brokers.
   The asking price is just a starting point.

3. Automobile dealers.
   Big automobile dealers can afford to take less profit per car than can the smaller dealers, but any dealer will talk price.

4. One-man operations.
   A farmer, a signpainter, a dressmaker, a TV repairman, and many others set their own price. Talk business!

5. Men bidding one against the other.
   The contractor in competition with other contractors for a job, the banker in competition with other bankers for a mortgage, the housepainter, the boy who mows the lawn, the actor—will *automatically* talk business.

When you make a beginning offer, *make an offer that makes sense*. The seller may not accept your offer but he will not be offended. With an offer that makes no sense at all, you have no starting place ... unless you are dealing with children. (Charles, Prince of Wales, once sold his English compositions written at school in Scotland to a classmate for $4.20, after which they fell into the hands of a Lancashire press agency. The agency sold the compositions to a German magazine for $28,000.)

Five steps to take to make a good bargain

1. Admire the merchandise.

2. Let the seller know that *you* know the market for this product or service.

3. Make a firm offer for less than you hope to pay but not so low as to be impossible.

4. Hold out some bait of your own. (Tell the real estate broker you will let him sell the lots you expect to sell when you buy the acreage you've been dickering for; tell the automobile dealer about your brother, also in the market for a car, etc.)

5. Once you've started negotiations, make it plain that you won't pay the full price. Be willing to walk away if you can't come to terms.

20

Accept Free Merchandise

(with trading stamps, coupons or as prizes)

The word *free* never grows old.

Look through any national magazine. "*Free*—for this *first volume* on France." (The advertiser here believes that you will not be able to resist the *second* volume.) "*Free*—a small bottle of vitamins when you purchase a large bottle!" (Come-on to get you to buy.) "*Free*—a new automobile if the number printed on this page is a lucky number. Take it to your dealer and find out." (Traffic builder for the dealer.) Are these offers dishonest? *Of course not.* Because every item announced as free is free.

Take free merchandise that you can use. "There is so much to say about Las Vegas, we can't possibly say it all here, so send for our free booklet," says the ad. If you are planning a trip to Las Vegas, send for the free booklet. That makes sense. "Register at your dealer's and get a free trip to Paris for two." If you're near the dealer's, register. *Somebody* gets those free prizes.

Many persons do not take what is coming to them. Take the prizes you get with stamps from the grocery store. One of the reasons the stamp outfits make such enormous profits is that 10% of all stamps are never turned in.

The store or filling station that gives you trading stamps *buys* them. So merchandise is marked up. Surely if you are paying for marked up merchandise you should trade in your stamps.

A merchandising man at Martex towels told us that one of the big stamp companies was the best customer he had. Bigger than any of the big chain or department stores or specialty shops. The stamp company buying towels in quantity can get them at a big discount. You can get china, draperies, and aluminum wear this way too. The premiums you get are good. So if you don't trade in your stamps, give them to someone who will. (We give ours to an aunt. Right now she's torn between buying a Lenox swan centerpiece for her table (3½ books) or waiting until she can buy a table lamp she has her eye on (4¾ books). We get our joy out of her letters.) Get your Christmas gifts with stamps.

Mort Weisinger wrote a book called "1001 Valuable Things You Can Get FREE" which is now in its fourth edition. One of the rules he sets forth for getting things free is to respect certain special conditions which may be stipulated. "If a self-addressed, stamped envelope is requested," he said, "send one." If there is a slight charge for mailing and handling costs, do not ignore this stipulation; remember, you're getting something valuable *free*. If the condition states that you must be a businessman, doctor, teacher, or member of a community organization to qualify for the free material, use your office stationery to prove your eligibility."

This makes good sense.

Our dentist friend has a drawer in his bathroom filled with samples of toothpaste, headache tablets, mouthwashes, toothbrushes and other oral products. Manufacturers hope he will recommend their products. If you are a professional man or a specialist in any field, you are eligible to get many free products. Send through professional magazines for the samples you want.

If you have moved into a new community, you have probably received a free basket from the Welcome Wagon. It operates like this. The merchant who gives you a gift pays to participate. 50 percent of his payment goes to the hostess, 50 percent to the parent company. (One automobile merchant gives the hostess a free car to drive so that you will see his car when it drives up in front to offer you a free carwashing at his garage.) The local beauty shop and barber shop pays to be able to give you a free gift because they want an introduction to you. So do others, so don't hesitate to call the Welcome Wagon if you move into a new community and get missed for some reason or other.

Sometimes gifts come free when you send in an unsolicited fan letter to a manufacturer. One of our daughters popped a can of popcorn at a slumber party she was having. "This is the best popcorn in the world," all the girls said. Later Susan said, "I'll never use any other kind of popcorn when I have a party."

"Tell that to the president of the company," we said, "and he'll probably send you a whole *case* of popcorn." Susan did write to the company out in Iowa, and told the president about her party. Not to her surprise, but to ours, she did, indeed, receive a whole case of popcorn.

You can't depend on getting a case of the product every time you write a fan letter. But true appreciation is always warmly received.

21

Go to the Source

Some Americans order roast beef in Marseille, the *bouillabaisse* [1] capital of the world. These are the tourists who bring home souvenir ash trays from world fairs.

Others are like our Kansas friends who stopped with us on their way home from the recent New York Fair. From the Indonesian Pavilion they had mugs made of Banka Tin (a new discovery in metalware that looks like polished pewter but is non-tarnishable) for $2.50 per mug; from the Sudan exhibit they brought tiny objects of hand-carved ivory (said to be the finest in the world) for $1.50; at the Swiss Pavilion they had picked up cowbells for $5.75 apiece (more than buying either direct or by mail from Switzerland but certainly more interesting than a foil unisphere made by a New York novelty house). They had carved panels of monkey pod wood from the Philippines, a wood horse from Sweden, a sari of pure silk with threads of gold from India, some hand-carved mahogany masks from Africa. Learn what is made where and you will find exceptional bargains. They did!

Once on a Caribbean cruise, an island-hopping couple joined our ship in Trinidad. Their take-home gifts included perfume from Martinique which had cost less than perfume on the Rue de la Paix; Delftware and orange-scented liqueurs from the Dutch island of Curacoa, (where diamonds are tagged at Amsterdam mark-downs); English tweeds from the British Island of St. Kitts.

---

[1] Fish stew.

Contrast this couple to the two who sat down for a bridge game
when we left our ship on a one-day stopover in Aruba. Hours
later when we returned (with a really superb Rembrandt reproduction on a foot square slab of beaverboard for $1), we found
the foursome still at it. The Rembrandt looks great in our hallway,
but then we didn't make four spades that day, doubled and
vulnerable.

The last time we traveled to Europe, each of us was allowed to
bring in $100 worth of duty-free merchandise, estimated at its
wholesale cost. (Custom officers appraised each item at no more
than half what we paid retail.) As of October 1st, 1965, customs
officers are estimating duty on the retail, not the wholesale, price.
But even now, a married couple can buy the equivalent of $800
worth of merchandise for the $200 spent at the source for mer-
chandise to be brought in duty-free. (Native products bought at
the source cost about ¼ of what they cost as imports in expensive
stores.) And here is a very important point to keep in mind.
*Except for tailor-made clothes and liquor, all merchandise brought
in is appraised at the wholesale cost after the first $100 worth is
appraised at retail.*

Visitors to St. Thomas before the new customs rule went into
effect, were spending from $20 to $100 on purchases there; to
San Juan about $25 to $75, not half as much as they were then
allowed to bring in duty free. So what do they come home with?
Straw hats? Baskets? St. Thomas is one of the finest shopping
centers in the world. Certainly, if you go there, come home with
all the duty free merchandise you are entitled to *and more*. Even
when you pay duty, you pay only on the wholesale price so you
pay less than when you buy the same merchandise at home with
the store's mark up added.

Travelers who don't limit themselves to their allowable quota
of duty-free merchandise are the ones who bring home treasures.
We saw an American shopper in Amsterdam, ordering a large
shaggy rug of colored wool. This fine example of Dutch craftsmanship contained 2200 miles of wool strands dyed in 12 orange and
deep red shades. Another American there was open-mouthed.

"Think of the duty you will have to pay," she said to the shopper. "I may never be in Amsterdam again," said the shopper, "and think of how proud I'll be of this 10 years from now."

In this book we cannot take you around the world telling you what is the best buy in every particular place. But we do urge you to follow these rules before going someplace new.

1. Read extensively about native skills and crafts.

2. Go to your local museum and look at treasures there.

3. Read any history that you have time to read.

4. If you are traveling by ship, attend the "briefing" usually conducted before stopping at a new port.

5. On a plane talk to persons returning to their own country. Talk to the stewardess. Read everything in the seat pocket about your destination.

Your trip will be more enjoyable, and you will come home with superb buys.

From Hawaii you will surely bring home handsome wooden salad bowls on legs; from Norway, enamel jewelry; from Bangkok, pearls and Dynasty silk suits; from Hong Kong, Temple rubbings (for around $3); from Denmark, clean-lined furniture for which you will pay far less than if you bought it here; from France, you may bring a Peugeot car. And you will know how to buy to save money at customs. You will ship your pearls unknotted and without a clasp. They will thus be classified as *unstrung* and the duty will be 5% rather than 55% (necklace duty). You will have the trademark taken off your perfume in Paris and so bring in many bottles of your favorite brand; you will contact a company like Cars Overseas in Paris and buy a French car tax-free in Paris, use it on your trip, then bring it home as a used car. (You save 22% in French taxes this way, and you get your car into the States at a used-car customs rate. Typical savings—$400 on a Peugeot 404 . . . plus transportation savings in Europe.) If you prefer a Fiat, buy that in Italy. A Volkswagen? Get that in Germany.

Want to buy a poodle in France, a dachshund in Germany, a

Scottie in Scotland? A personal pet not imported for sale can be included in your customs exemption. If your purchases exceed the amount, a monkey, cat, or dog will be charged at 7½ percent of its value; canaries at 10% of their value. Check Customs for shipping and quarantine regulations. (Regulations are not complicated, but can be bothersome if you don't think ahead.)

Buying at the source in the United States

There is a great push for travel business at home. Because of this we will get less duty-free exemptions when buying overseas, but we will benefit with greater promotion of "at the source" products here.

In Maine, at the lobster pounds (where live lobsters are kept in pots in salt water), shellfish can be bought *and shipped* for far less than you can buy them in non-salt water areas. Wool blankets woven at the Amana colonies near Iowa City, Iowa are great bargains, and bologna which is a specialty at Iowa's Dutch colony at Pella is a delicacy. Wisconsin cheeses (some with Caraway seeds) will be shipped from the cheese stores in that state. The Flemington area in New Jersey has many glass and pottery outlets where seconds are sold. All the fine glassware plants in West Virginia sell seconds at half price. (Glass plants are in Milton, Morgantown, New Martinsville, Williamstown, Huntington, and Weston.)

In a letter from Richard Bittman, Industrial Economist for the Department of Development in New Mexico (State Capitol, Santa Fe), we have word about "an unusual manufacturing firm which produces a specialized line of high quality aluminum cookware, bowls, and ash trays in modern design with a plant fifteen miles north of Santa Fe at Projoaque, New Mexico, which offers ⅓ off on all items purchased at the plant which do not meet the firm's high standards.

Mr. Bittman also reminded us that Indian artifacts, sterling, turquoise jewelry, and handwoven rugs are available at all of New Mexico's Indian reservations at substantial savings.

If you are a builder, you probably know what materials are available at low cost in your state. If you are remodeling your own house, you too should know. In South Dakota, forestry products can be purchased at the source for a big price reduction; at sawmills in the Black Hills, posts, poles, and rough lumber are bargains. Slabs of granite can be purchased for less at quarries in Vermont. Fieldstone can be bought from farmers in the New England states who have fields divided with old stone fences. Lime to sweeten the soil can be picked up at the limestone quarry in Sussex County in New Jersey. It's sold at about cost.

Do you know the wreckers in your town? Go to them if you want window frames—old storm windows—a circular stairway—a fireplace mantle. They collect and sell locally. If you want a stained glass window or a handsome newell post, keep your eyes open for buildings about to come down. Find the wrecker, go to him ordering your "piece of the building" in advance. Sometimes, wreckers will *give* you merchandise, other times you pay.

Farmers invite you to come to the source when crops become more abundant than they can harvest. Orchards near Brewster, New York, let you pick peaches there for less than a dollar a bushel, owners of strawberry patches in North Carolina let you pick your own strawberries for 80% off the market price, apple growers in the state of Washington have similar rules.

You will not take time to pick fruit when travelling, but certainly you can know what specialties are available. Send home a crate of citrus fruits from Florida; it is priced about the same as it is priced at your local grocery store but it is better quality fruit. Send salt water taffy home from Atlantic City, pralines from New Orleans, a ham from Virginia.

Look for artists near you

Many residents near Cedar Rapids, Iowa found themselves with priceless paintings just 20 years after Grant Wood first began selling his work. Dave Turner, owner of a mortuary there, was one of the first to recognize his talent. To help him get started, he bought every painting the artist wanted to sell him, even provided young Grant with a home. (Today the Turner collection is famous.) Gardner Cowles, owner of the Des Moines *Register* and *Look* magazine bought two of Wood's first paintings for $75 each. Chicago Art Institute paid only $300 for "American Gothic."

Take note of all artists around you. Is there a photographer who is beginning to get national recognition? Commission him to take a picture of your home or child. Is there someone doing woodcarving, a craftsman making unusual pieces of furniture, a weaver duplicating old designs in a rug, a young couple specializing in ceramics?

Follow the artist who wins a prize or has his things accepted for an exhibit. What you buy now may soon be priceless.

In Plainfield, near Waterloo, Iowa, Ruth Roach is winning national acclaim for her hand-crafted jewelry. Arts festivals and museums wait for her one-of-a-kind necklaces, pins, and bracelets which have their clasps and chains incorporated into the integral part of the design. Still relatively inexpensive (a small pregnant bird in silver entitled "Gloria Wait For Me" costs $17.50), this is the kind of work that will increase in value as further recognition comes.

Seek out the source where unusual products are made, whatever those products may be.

Part Three

How to cut back expenses

in ten vital areas

1

Your Home or Apartment

By following one of the three plans below, you can live for nothing.

PLAN A: Divide your home so that someone pays you rent which in turn pays your expenses. (*Example:* Make a duplex.)

PLAN B: Live free in *another's* home in exchange for performing a service. (*Example:* Get a job as governess for Elizabeth Taylor's children. Live free as part of her entourage.)

PLAN C: Live near your work with all expenses paid as part of your way of life. (*Example:* Live in quarters on a U. S. Army base).

Plan A

If you have a large home, rent three upstairs bedrooms to school teachers. The income will pay your taxes and some household expenses.

Or, instead of renting three separate bedrooms, rent a whole floor. Give each teacher a bedroom, but now make a fourth bedroom into a living room complete with a writing desk, TV, sofas, a record player, good paintings and low lamps. The teachers will pay more for this suite.

Or make your upstairs into an apartment, complete with

kitchen. The investment will take capital and your heat bill and taxes will go up, but if there is a demand in your town for apartments (either furnished or unfurnished) this investment will pay for itself. As you get income you will be allowed depreciation for your original investment on your income tax.

OTHER POSSIBILITIES

- If you have a barn on your property, convert it to a home. Furnish it effectively with things from auctions or second hand stores, and rent it. Borrow from the bank for your conversion, pay off your mortgage with the income you get from rent. The difference between the mortgage payment and your rent should pay for *your* living.
- If you are living on property with a site for a second home, investigate pre-fab homes through your local dealer. They are no longer flimsy, and you can get a full mortgage in most cases when you put one on your property. The income will pay for your mortgage. (You may wonder if it is wiser to sell such a home or rent it. Our accountant says *rent*. You will get a tax benefit and at the same time your property will be appreciating. Property in most sections of the country is going up every year.)
- If you have a summer home in the north, a winter home in the south, rent both. Rent your northern home in the winter to school teachers. Rent your summer home at *off-season rates* to graduate students working in the south on a summer project.
- If you have a parcel of land with no house on it, sell off a piece. Use this money as a down payment on a house you can build. If you do not want a pre-fab house, get a construction mortgage. (You will have to take plans for your home to the bank, but you will be given a mortgage as high as 80% of the estimated cost of your house. You will not get this money all at one time, but at three stages of construction someone from the bank will approve construction, charging your account about $15 a call.) Once the building is up, your taxes will go up, but you will receive rent which will pay for your mortgage. Eventually you

will have a home in the country completely paid for. Then, you can move in. Many couples looking toward retirement buy a house this way.

- Even if you own no property, you can live for free. Instead of renting one apartment, rent *two*. Furnish both and sublet *one* at a rent higher than what you pay for it unfurnished. (Be sure to tell your landlord in writing exactly what you plan to do. Then he can have no objection later.) The profit you make from your second apartment can pay for your apartment.

(When Clarence Darrow, famous for the defense in the Loeb-Leopold trial, took his bride to their first apartment in South Side Chicago, he rented not one but two apartments in the same building. When he died he was still on the lease for two apartments; the subletting of the second paid for most of the rent for his own apartment for most of his married life.)

At one time we were on the lease as tenants for five apartments in various buildings in New York. We rented them unfurnished, then furnished them from auctions, subletting them at a good profit. The profit more than paid for the rent of our duplex. There is an obvious risk. Should your apartments go unrented, the monthly rent you are obligated to pay is a large one. Be sure that there is a big market for furnished apartments in your city before you contemplate this.

When you rent an apartment to furnish and sublet, get one with a good location. Then make it look, feel, and smell like home. Two types rent furnished apartments. The first is irresponsible; he will sign anything and live anywhere. (You don't want him. Skipping out from a furnished apartment is easy to do.) The second is responsible but temporarily displaced. He may be getting a divorce. Or he may be a transferred executive whose wife has stayed behind to sell their home and get the children through school. (His company pays for the apartment and he is an excellent renter.) Or you may rent to a city executive who brings his wife in from the suburbs for the winter theater season. Or you may rent to three pilots or three stewardesses. (They are in and out of a city so much they have no time to furnish an apartment, and they are ideal renters.)

- Trade your home for a home. A few years ago Betty Ostroff got an idea for a Vacation Exchange Club. The cost for joining the club, at 554 Fifth Avenue, New York City, is $5. Write there for a list of homes. Join and you can exchange your home for one of comparable value. You decide whether you want to go to California or Hawaii or Florida for several months. Then, you write to someone on the list who has a home you think you would like to live in. If that person wants to spend the months you want to spend in his home in exchange for the same months in your home, you are in business. California and New York do the most exchanging, Mrs. Ostroff says.
- Trade a service for a home. A widow living near us lets a young couple live free in her home under these conditions: (1) She reserves a bedroom and bath for her personal use at all times. (She travels much, has an apartment in New York, but wants to come to the country whenever she feels like it.) (2) She reserves the right to take over the house during the months of the year at any given notice. (The couple can continue to stay there but now *they* take the room and bath, while she takes over the house.) (3) The couple maintains the house as they would their own, but the owner hires an occasional gardener and cleaning woman.

If you have no children, look for this kind of trade. You can live for nothing as you save money for the home you want.

A young college friend went to Italy in an exchange program from Syracuse University. She arranged her semester exchange in the spring in order to spend the summer in Europe. For three months she served as a governess in a wealthy home in Florence. Her living was free.

Sublet the apartment you live in when you go away on vacation or have to be out of town for a few months. The only risk you take is that your renters will be careless. Choose your tenants carefully, and don't be too fussy about things. The added income will more than offset the breaking of an ash tray or even of a table. (Sublet and have your own rent paid, plus a profit for renting furnished.)

Do you like the role of landlord? Some do, some don't. A few years ago a woman executive in New York whose two children were in boarding school, agreed to take a large apartment with two other business women. The lease appeared so formidable to her two associates that they refused to sign. With some fear, she signed alone, renting a third of the apartment to each of the other two. Eventually, her two tenants drifted away, but others came, and now she charged more per person. Within two years, each of her two "tenants" paid for 50% of the apartment. What's more, they were suburban women who stayed in the apartment on week nights only. The woman executive's children came home from school on weekends. If you welcome responsibility, by all means let this trait pay off for you. If not, live free in *another's* home.

Plan B

If you have children, your family can live on a farm that you may run for someone, or at a ranch. But possible trades are not numerous. A single person can work as a secretary, governess, or overseer of a career woman's home in exchange for room and board, or she can be a public relations gal at a resort, or he can work as an assistant to the cruise director on a ship or as a ski instructor at a lodge. If you are single and want to live for nothing, figure out what you can trade and where you want to live. Then, do it.

Plan C

In many states, if you are worried about supporting yourself in old age, you can will your home to the state. The state will pay your taxes and, often, some other expenses, for life. Colleges will make this same arrangement.

Perhaps you prefer to make this deal with one of your children.

Many parents do. (An Idaho couple was unable to maintain their ranch. One son said, "I know you prefer to live here rather than to live with us. I will pay all expenses, maintaining the ranch as you have always maintained it, but in exchange I want the money I spend during the years ahead to be compensated for in your will." Cold? No! This is just common sense.) Talk cold turkey to your children, and vice versa.

There are now many homes for the aged in which the resident buys a suite, an apartment or a cottage in a Senior Citizens colony. Once bought, the residence of the person is insured for life (or should be) no matter what that person's physical condition may eventually be.

In making a lifetime deal with members of your family, a residential club, or your state, itself, get the advice of a lawyer.

Sometimes your housing comes as part payment for the work you do. The Army provides a home on a post for an officer and his family, providing one with more bedrooms as new babies arrive. (Quarters become more elegant as the officer progresses in rank.) Other branches of the military offer similar inducements, and several other branches of the government provide housing for persons overseas. The Peace Corps provides housing; large corporations provide homes for employees sent to foreign countries; internes are given free quarters in some hospitals; nurses often pay nothing for their quarters; the Red Cross provides housing for its members in many parts of the world.

When you go to work, do not consider money alone. If housing is provided, the job may be worth three times what it appears to be at first glance. For one thing, your taxes will not be as high. Food costs, as well as other expenses, are cut way down.

Other low cost arrangements

- Expense Accounts. The single person traveling on an expense account benefits more than do the heads of families, whose expenses go on just the same. When you travel on company expense, arrange your vacation to coincide with a trip.

A company that transfers you expects to pay moving expenses. This usually includes living expenses in a new city until your family gets there. Sometimes a company will buy your home so that you can get the new one you want.

Wise home buying

If you plan to live only a few years in a house, buy with as large a mortgage as you can get. Pay taxes and insurance with mortgage payments, but pay no more per month than you would for rent. Your aim: to sell for at least what you paid for the house, plus what you have paid out per month. Do this, and you will have lived for nothing.

Shopping for a mortgage

If you are buying for life, get the best interest rate you can get on a mortgage, and pay as much down on a home as you can afford to pay. Development owners often advertise "nothing down." They can usually get a buyer 80% of his purchase price at 6% mortgage from a bank. They will then offer to give the remaining 20% of the purchase price in a second mortgage which *they* will carry at 10%. "Nine times out of 10," one developer told us, "the buyer will raise the cash rather than pay that 10% for a second mortgage." The "no cash down" is an advertising gimmick.

If you are eligible for an FHA mortgage, borrow money at 5¼% interest (plus ½% for insurance of the money) from a lender approved by the Federal Housing Administration. If you are eligible for a GI loan, you can get a direct loan from the Veterans Administration up to $15,000 or can have 60% of your loan guaranteed by a bank or other lender. Such government insured mortgages are advantageous when you do not have much money to pay down on a house (you need pay nothing down with a GI loan), and need a long time to pay off your mortgage (20 to 30 years).

When borrowing from a bank, you will usually be allowed to borrow up to twice your gross annual income. (If your income is

$18,000, you can borrow $36,000 from a bank.) Be sure to get a letter saying that you can pay off your loan as rapidly as you want with no penalty and can have monthly payments adjusted whenever you make a prepayment of principal of $500 or more.

If you are eligible, use an FHA loan for home construction. The cost is less than for a straight bank loan. Even so, an FHA loan at 5¼% costs you about 10% in annual interest cost. Mortgage interest is deductible at tax time.

Saving on utilities

Gas, electricity, and telephone are basic expenses. Consider them as part of your overall household expenses. And be sure to understand what you are paying for. In New York City you are allowed 75 local (one message unit) calls for $5.60 a month, plus tax. You can talk all day on one call and not be charged more. Hang up and call again and your bill begins to go up.

When you order a telephone for the first time, you often must deposit as much as $60. The company pays you 4% interest on this money, returning it when credit is established. Buy a color telephone once for $10 and you are credited for life for this telephone wherever you live. (Personally, we think by now the black telephone is the chic one.)

Check changing time rates when making a long distance call. Call Los Angeles from New York from 4:30AM to 6PM, station to station any weekday and you pay $2; from 6PM to 8PM that same day $1.50; from 8PM to 4:30AM, $1. (This is the same principle as "off season" fares when traveling by ship, only the cut is better. Fares for all classes on ships are usually cut about 10%.)

If you are going away from New York for about two months but want your same number when you return, have your phone temporarily disconnected. If someone dials your number, the operator will give your present number, even if it is way across the continent. The price is $5 for five months; and after that, $1 a month. (Pay the basic charge for two months and you pay $11.20; pay this way and you pay $5.) There is no service charge for reconnecting your phone. Check your business office for local prices.

The reason consumers (women, especially) are confused about telephone and utility bills is because of the wordage. Message units, cubic feet of gas, killowatts—what do they mean? All are simply units of measurements as bananas are measurements in a bunch of bananas. The more "bananas" you burn the less you pay for each. If you have few electric appliances, you pay 4 cents a kilowatt hour; electric heat and lots of appliances, the cost can go down to 1½ cents an hour. For gas, your meter registers the pressure in a cubic foot of gas. In New York you are allowed to burn a minimum of 10 electric killowatts for 100 hours for $1.50 per month; 300 cubic feet of gas for $1.50. Go away and you can have your service discontinued and save $3.00 a month. In New York, when you order gas and electric service, you pay a $20 deposit. When you discontinue this service, you get this back with 6% interest.

2

Household Furnishings

The readers of confession magazines are practical.

They do not read a daily newspaper, they are not well informed about world events, and they read love stories to escape from the tough realities of everyday life. But they buy furniture sensibly. As they prepare for marriage, they purchase first a comfortable double bed; second, a big refrigerator. All other furniture comes later.

These young women do not elope. They accept a round of showers before marriage. This way they start out with linens for the bed they buy and good utensils for the kitchen.

Once their basic needs are provided for, the fancy things can come. As one homemaking editor told us, "They consider a good stove fancy. They can cook on a bunch of sticks. But that refrigerator! That is of great psychological importance."

If you or one of your children is getting married, make sure that life begins with a good bed and refrigerator. But do not buy *on time*.

Let's say the refrigerator costs $420. Pay $36 a month for it for the next three years and you pay an interest rate of over 40%. Too much! Save up for the refrigerator before buying or borrow at a true 6%, then buy.

Hopefully, you newlyweds will not insist on a new refrigerator. (Every two seconds a major appliance is taken out of someone's home to make room for a new one. Get one of these "still good" appliances for one-fourth the price.)

Certainly you will not buy your bed on time. Insist on the best mattress and pillows (the best being the most comfortable), but get your bed at a second-hand place and refinish or antique it.

Large refrigerators, like large TV sets, can be bought at auctions, especially firemen's auctions in the country. These outsize objects are donated by widows or retired couples now moving to smaller homes. If you dislike second-hand things, but want to save money on a good model, go to a Railway Salvage place. There you can get a new refrigerator which may have been dented in transit for far less than the price for a new model.

If you *do* buy *new* insist on a warranty and mail it in. And don't pay for gadgets!

Basic furniture buying plan

Divide your furnishings into three classifications.

1. Bed, mattresses, bedding, refrigerator, big towels, a newspaper delivered to your door, a good lighted mirror in your bathroom, a good chair to read in, a good reading light, good cooking utensils, a TV that works if this constitutes entertainment, a great fireplace.

2. *Furnishings that you have to have:* A furnace, adequate plumbing, a good roof, a typewriter if you use it for work, an automobile if you need it to get places in, a table, tableware, chairs, chests of drawers, a clock, a fenced-in yard if you have children or a dog.

3. *Furnishings you want:* Good paintings, good floor coverings, good tableware, handsome lamps, beautiful furniture and appointments, wallpaper, curtains, sterling silver.

Work toward items in the first group *first*. If you are buying a home, you will also have to buy many of the items in group *two*. (Here you have to be sure that everything *works*.) Group *three* items can be purchased over the years, and may be replaced as your taste becomes more sophisticated.

30 rules for wise furniture buying

1. Never buy *sets*. (Furniture need not match but it must harmonize. Sets are merchandising gimmicks, most often offered for sale by installment houses. Shun especially *big* sets—"19 piece home starter sets"—which have rugs, lamps and end tables put in.)

2. Avoid buying in installment stores which charge interest on the unpaid balance of your bill. You not only pay high for your credit, you pay more for the furniture, too.

3. Go to the basement *first*, when buying in a department store. (For promotional reasons, there is less margin of profit made on goods sold here.)

4. Work out a buying plan. Then, you can watch for sales, price wars and clearances, getting what you want the minute you see it at a good price.

5. Buy classic furniture. (Simple furniture will not be "dated" in a hurry; also, the money that has gone into such furniture has gone for construction and good materials, not for fancy-work.)

6. Watch for price wars. (You will have to read competitive advertising of two stores to recognize a war when you see one. But once you see two advertisers (usually in Chicago, New York, or Philadelphia or some other large city) alternately reducing the price of say, a breakfast room table and four chairs, you can get a real bargain. Sometimes, to win on the battlefield, one store comes down to *wholesale* price.)

7. Go to annual sales of furniture—occurring all over the nation in February and August. Mark-downs will not be 30% off regular price, but mark-downs will be great because the store wants the promotion that comes from advertising better-than-average savings. One or two "leaders" will be marked down *below* 30%.

8. Look for *special purchase* sales. Watch TV or listen to radio for appeals of discount houses. These houses exist by buying great quantities of radios, TV sets, washing machines, or anything else, and offering them at bargain prices for fast clearance. Good buys here.

9. Go to clearance sales for bulky or highly promoted items like lawn tables and umbrellas. Mark-downs come at the end of the season when winter storage is a problem.

10. Go to the basement for *last* year's promotion color (orange, purple or whatever) in a White Sale. For quality merchandise similar to what is upstairs, prices will be down.

11. Shop for specifics. Carry samples of your colors with you, measurements of your furniture.

12. Shop for "private brands" on items like vacuum cleaners—the store brand may be the same as a nationally promoted brand —the price will be much less.

13. Look for seconds or irregulars in carpeting, use these "imperfects" wisely—place rugs where pulled threads and blemished places will not get great wear.

14. Watch out for tricks. "Everything on 4th floor at half price." The *beautiful* things may be taken off the floor before the sale. Watch out for "list prices" that are fictitious, etc. You will get to see tricks when you have done comparison shopping.

15. Use books as a decoration and entertainment in your home. Buy them at way down prices in second-hand book shops.

16. Select auctions wisely for particular merchandise. (Example: At an auction where lower-to-middle class people are buying, beds will go *high*. But at a gallery specializing in antique books, a custom-made bed may go for as little as $5 or $10. The buyers are interested in a collector's item, not in a second-hand bed.)

17. Buy with a group—your company or a buying club—to get merchandise for less. A group buying 10 sewing machines will get a better price for members than will one person buying one sewing machine.

18. Watch for sample houses that don't advertise. Manufacturers do not supply "samples" to advertisers who compete with their regular customers. Therefore, a sample house that advertises all kinds of samples is probably a phony.

19. Study the "fliers" sent out by mail order houses. These are clearance sheets and offer cut prices on merchandise already priced low.

20. Buy antiques on the highway rather than in a high rent district if you really know antiques, not if you don't.

21. If you hate your floors and decide you have to buy carpeting to cover these floors, *wait.* You may have a prettier floor if you lay down wide stained planks, especially if your home is an old home and wide floorboards look authentic.

22. Buy Oriental rugs at auctions, also odd shades of carpeting. Real buys come where dealers buy, not where dealers sell.

23. Whenever possible, make your own slip covers and draperies —or select a fabric and hire a seamstress to make them, not a decorator's shop.

24. Buy draperies at estate auctions. Beautiful lined draperies often go for as little as $10 a pair, and can be shortened for your needs.

25. When having furniture moved, have your things insured through the mover. (To determine cost of moving, multiply total weight by $1.25 a pound.) Insurance is good for 60 days, and allows for storage.

26. If you are being transferred by your company, expect your organization to pay for moving. When paying for your own moving, use a trailer whenever possible. Do-it-yourself moving is a great money-saver.

27. Study periods of furniture before seeking good buys in antiques.

28. Before picking up a "buy" in sheets rub one between your fingers over a dark cloth. Does white powder come off? Your sheet has sizing in it. Allowable sizing is 6%. More than this, and your sheet will be limp and weak after the first washing.

29. Do not buy fabrics where you have furniture recovered. Buy your fabric yourself at a mill end shop or other cut-rate place. Shop until you get a good price for the making of slipcovers.

30. If you have a legitimate irritation when you shop, *complain.* Store managers say you don't (not nearly enough), and the future of their business depends on their knowing what you object to as well as what you want.

3

The Big Nut:
Food, Tobacco, and Beverages

A few years ago, Alfred Politz Research, Inc. interviewed 10,000 families across the nation and found they spent their money in these eight categories: (1) food, tobacco, and beverages, (2) clothing, (3) medical and personal care, (4) home operation, improvement, (5) home furnishings and equipment, (6) recreation and recreation equipment, (7) automobile, (8) other, e.g., life insurance, premiums, misc. *Food, Tobacco, and Beverages* is the number one expenditure for all families. Researchers say this should be even higher. (Interviewees prefer to understate actual expenses for liquor, making for minor error.)

The Politz study served as background for the New York *Herald Tribune's* series, *"How I Spend My Money."* One report was on a cab driver and his working wife, whose combined take-home pay was $7800.

George drove his cab 10 hours a night (when tips are 50% higher and the traffic is less of a push) and Martha worked in a dress shop. George took home $5200 a year; Martha, $2600. They supported an invalid sister and a teen-age daughter. (One son, married, was on his own.)

George's hobby, in his own words, was "my daughter." Peggy had a $100 typewriter, a $125 portable TV set, a $90 portable record player, a $40 portable radio, a summer camp for $650 a summer. Her teeth were straight due to long-time orthodontia, and her clothes were carefully selected by her mother. As Martha explained, "She's a young girl, and she has to have a nice appearance or it may affect her chances later on."

George and Martha had one interest outside of Peggy: *"big, old-fashioned family dinners."* Said Martha, "My relatives don't have any hobbies. They just eat. We don't drink." George and Martha spent $250 a month on food.

If yours is an average family, you spend 40% or more of your income on food. Food manufacturers say that because demand for food is greater than for any other commodity, food manufacturers and retailers can take less profit and still stay in business. (They point to profits of 2.4% as opposed to 3.1% for other manufacturers. From 1947 through 1964, prices of other commodities increased 35%; food, only 25%.) But in April, 1965, the Labor Department reported a sharp turn upward in food prices. Meat, potatoes, strawberries, apples, green peppers, and cucumbers went way up. So did eggs, but this is a typical occurrence at Easter. If food goes up and your income remains the same you are in trouble unless you find ways to buy for less.

Give up synthetic vitamins and/or other supplements

Vitamins are unnecessary if you eat a well-balanced diet. So if you are buying vitamins because you think that your family needs them, you are reacting as manufacturers want you to react. Unless a doctor has found that you have a specific deficiency, you can get all the vitamins, minerals, and protein you need daily by eating these foods, considered essential by the Department of Agriculture.

> Milk, for a child ¾ to 1 quart; for an adult, 1 pint; or cheese
> Leafy vegetables—1 serving or more
> Tomatoes, oranges, grapefruit—1 serving or more
> Other vegetables or fruit—2 or more servings
> Eggs, lean meat, poultry or fish—1 serving or more
> Enriched cereals or bread—2 servings

Butter or margarine—2-3 tablespoons
Sugar—for energy.

Eat a well-balanced diet, and you won't need vitamin pills or reducing pills.

Simple way to save

Write down what you think you spend for food every month. Add to it any spending you do for pills that help you gain weight, lose weight, or pep you up. Has your food bill gone up 1%, 3%, 5%?

For the next three months don't buy dietary supplements not recommended by your doctor. You will save what you have been spending on pills, but by eating a good basic diet you will have a real reduction in your food bills, too. You will have less desire for expensive snacks, soft drinks, and candy. Good basic food is satisfying food. The first step toward wiser buying is wiser eating.

Be an informed consumer

Thousands of dollars are spent each year by government and business to tell you how to buy, how to use, and how to care for food.

Here are just a few of the free books that are offered:

Use Your Freezer Every Day	Dow Chemical Co., Consumer Education 690 Building Midland, Michigan
Meal Planning Guide	Pet Milk Company Arcade Building St. Louis, 66, Mo.
Food for the Family *How to Control Your Weight*	Metropolitan Life Insurance Co. 1 Madison Avenue New York, N. Y.
Family Fare *Food for Fitness* *Money Saving Main Dishes* *Food for Your Weight*	Office of Information U. S. Department of Agriculture Washington 25, D. C.

Food for Your Family *Choose Your Calories Wisely*	Kellogg Company Home Economics Services Battle Creek, Michigan

Know Your Egg Law
Protection for Consumers—
  Weights & Measures
	N. Y. State Department of
	  Agriculture & Markets
	State Office Building
	Albany 1, N. Y.

Buying Food for Your Camp—
  #10
Buying Food for Your Nursing
  Home—#12
Buying Food for Your Family—
  #13
Buying Times for Fresh Fruits &
  Vegetables—#14
Buying Times for Meats—#16
Do You Know Food Labels?—
  #15
	N. Y. State Extension Service
	Food Marketing Information for
	  Consumers
	11 Park Place
	New York 7, N. Y.

The ABC's of Freezing *Outdoor Tips with Aluminum* *Foil*	Alcoa Wrap Public Relations Department 1501 Alcoa Building Pittsburgh, Penna.

Keep a shopping file just as you keep a recipe file. Write to the Department of Extension Teaching and Information of your State University for a listing of booklets available on recipes, canning, freezing, gardening, meal planning. (Cornell Extension Bulletin #47, which you can get free by writing to the Department of Extension Teaching and Information, N. Y. S. College of Agriculture, Ithaca, N. Y., lists over 100 home economics booklets with information about food, health, household management, child development and allied subjects.)

Ask your Home Demonstration Agent or Farm Bureau in your County Seat for a free listing of booklets on homemaking and farming.

Get the free listing of publications available from the U. S. Government, grouped by subject, from Superintendent of Documents, U. S. Government Printing Office, Washington 25, D. C.

Get the free list of available booklets from McCall's, Box 1390, Grand Central Station, New York 17, New York—the list of similar booklets available from Woman's Day, 67 West 54th Street, New York, N. Y.

Good Housekeeping, 57th Street & 8th Avenue offers a free list of products and services advertised in the magazine, will send you names recommended for any specific type of merchandise approved by the magazine. The American Home Economics Association, 1600 20th Street, N. W., Washington 9, D. C. has a list of publications that you can get free.

Do your homework

Appliance manufacturers say that consumers don't read instruction booklets. They do not defrost their refrigerators as instructed. They refreeze foods which should not be frozen twice. They broil meat with the doors of their electric ovens closed when the booklet specifies *open*.

To become a better shopper do your homework. Learn what low cost products have the same nutritional value as high cost products. Know how to read labels. Know weights and measures. Learn to use low cost cuts of meats.

Follow the price index as reported in your local newspaper. Know what foods are going up and coming down and why. Listen to radio reports from the extension division of an agricultural college. Find out what fruits and vegetables and other farm products are plentiful.

Plan your menus before you go to the store. Then follow these suggestions:

30 rules that will bring down the cost of food in your home

1. Buy in bulk or in large packages rather than in small packages. Get a large cheese which you slice yourself, rather than eight small slices, etc. Get sweet potatoes from a bin, not in small packages, etc.

2. Buy store brands.

3. Buy fresh fruits and vegetables in season; frozen or canned foods at other times.

4. Buy surplus commodities (as reported in radio market reports).

5. Buy different grades of foods for different purposes.

6. Do not spend more than 20 cents per $1.00 expenditures for store-bought baked goods.

7. When buying meat, buy the largest amount of *lean* meat for your price.

8. Buy anything; meat, potatoes, fruit, *anything,* with the intended use in mind. (Example: Don't make Swiss steak out of sirloin.)

9. Don't go *meat* mad! It's expensive! (Good rule—figure a quarter pound of meat per day for every adult in your family; figure ½ pound when buying with bone and fat.)

10. Use non-fat dried milk for cooking, instead of real milk. (Write the food processor which makes the dried milk you buy for free recipes.)

11. Unless you have an enormous family, do not pay for delivery of milk. If you buy at a good modern supermarket, delivery boys will load your car. Milk will keep for a week in your refrigerator.

12. Substitute low cost foods with equal food value in recipes calling for expensive products. (Less fancy grades for fancy grades, etc.)

13. Don't substitute *cream* cheese for a high protein food. (It has fillers and more water for spreadability. Cottage cheese is the best cheese for protein.)

14. Buy roasting chickens and turkey when buying poultry. They yield more meat in proportion to bone than do fryers, etc.

15. Grade B eggs are just as nutritious as Grade A eggs. There is no difference, either, in nutritional value of brown and white eggs.

16. Most fruits, vegetables, and melons have the most food value when they have the best flavor. Buy cantaloupe, peaches, pears, and strawberries when they are at their freshest and best. Do not buy in packages, if possible. Packages prevent inspection—you may find bad spots.

17. Buy fish when cheap. A pound of fish has as much food value as a pound of meat.

18. Cabbage and lettuce should be heavy for their size.

19. Dried fruits and vegetables are more economical than processed foods.

20. In checking contents of a can in your supermarket, figure that 8 oz. means ½ pound or one measuring cup.

21. Buy nuts by the bagful, not shelled and chopped.

22. Learn to identify different cuts of meat.

23. Check the price per pound when buying meat or anything sold by the pound, watch scales when buying, count change. Often a customer's indifference encourages a market to overcharge.

24. Use frozen foods immediately upon defrosting.

25. Store bread in your refrigerator.

26. Don't be afraid to store food in opened cans. Do cover, however.

27. Do not cook vegetables long before serving, and cook in small quantities of water to preserve vitamins.

28. Serve larger portions of fewer foods, rather than a *smorgasbord* of many foods at the same meal.

29. Plan your menus taking into account your family's preferences and storage space. Allow for alternates if your market is out of what you have in mind.

30. Consult a weight chart (provided by your insurance company) to find out the ideal weight for each member of your family. Subtly, take away calories from the fat members, and add calories for the thin ones. (Figure an average of 2,000 calories per adult to maintain weight, not losing or gaining.)

Food is more enjoyable when it is served with flair. Here are some suggestions for increasing appetite appeal:

1. Eat in different parts of your home, even if your home is not spacious. Serve lunch outdoors, dinner in front of the fire, a midnight snack at a counter in the kitchen. Surprise your family with an unexpected setting.

2. Don't differentiate between family meals and company meals. No company china! No company silver!

3. Provide the same basic nutritional elements every day, but not the same foods. Serve French Bread (cut at the table) instead of sliced bread one day, baked eggs instead of fried eggs on Sunday morning, a frothy surprise dessert. Keep sameness out of cooking by coming up with one "surprise" a day.

4. Serve new things. But don't rush to buy everything new you hear described in TV commercials. (Of the 8,000 products you have to choose from at a supermarket, two-thirds are new or have been improved in the last 10 years. Yet these are just a fraction of the new items that have been offered to consumers. 92% of the new products introduced each year are rejected and disappear.) Let someone else do the experimenting.

5. Serve a drink before dinner if you want to, but not more than two alcoholic drinks per person if you want guests to enjoy your food.

6. Order foreign food by mail either from shops in a large American city or from Europe. Request a cook book every time you order from someplace new.

7. Know your herbs. Get a catalogue from an herb house; also, a spice rack.

8. Use substitutes in recipes. (Honey for sugar, buckwheat instead of white flour, crabmeat instead of shrimp.) Make your own recipes.

9. Have at least three full-meal specialties that you know you do better than anyone else you know. (Baked beans with brown bread, maybe; home made vegetable soup and apple pie; lasagne.)

10. Serve unusual foods, picking up tricks when you travel. (For instance, the French scoop out the meat from lemons or oranges, pack with lemon ice and/or orange ice, seal the shell together and freeze. Dessert eaten from its "natural" container is inexpensive.)

11. Know how to use these five classes of wines: appetizer wines (sherry and vermouth); white table wines (sauterne and rhine); red table wines (claret and burgundy); sweet dessert wines (port, muscatel, tokay); and sparkling wines (champagne and sparkling burgundy).

12. Keep a jar of unusual candies in your home. (Buy the old-timers like clove drops, sour balls, licorice drops, etc.; they cost little, can take the place of a big dessert.)

Soft drinks, liquor, tobacco, and candies

1. Make your own soft drinks. Serve iced tea, flavored with mint or lemon; iced coffee with a cinnamon stick; old-fashioned lemonade; punch made with fruit juices blended in the blender. (Bottling and advertising bring up the cost of bottled drinks. Old-fashioned home drinks are *chic.*)

2. Bring back more than one quart of duty-free liquor when traveling. Wines bought at the source are inexpensive, and duty is low.

3. Do not give cocktail parties. Most people are now bored with stand-up drinking parties. Rather, give several small buffet dinners, serving only a minimum of cocktails. Your good food will be remembered far longer than liquor.

4. Try for *unusual* parties. A Sunday afternoon "talk" with sherry (from your last trip) as the refreshment. A Jamaican breakfast with rum used as a flavoring for iced fruit. An after-theatre party with ale mixed with iced tomato juice as the nightcap. Or serve champagne, brought in by the case (with a duty and internal revenue tax of only about 99 cents a bottle).

5. Quit smoking.

6. Bring cigarettes home duty-free for guests who insist, or bring home an allotment of good cigars (300 duty-free cigars allowed). If your neighboring state charges less cigarette tax than *your* state charges, bring in cigarettes by the carton.

7. Buy candies in bulk, not in a gift box. Buy broken candies for toppings, etc.

8. Make candy, box it yourself, and freeze. Your home-made fudge or divinity will be appreciated more than store candy.

In America we have 15 times as much food as anyone else. Learn the ways to enjoy this abundance without overpaying.

4

Clothes for Men

by Cle Kinney

(*Editor's Note:* Here's where the authors part company. Cle gives his views on the ideal wardrobe for men; Jean does the same for women. Cle talks first, because as Jean says, "Men pay the bills.")

As an American male, you lean toward one of three ways of dressing. You tend to dress like (1) *a successful American business man;* or (2) *a graduate of an Ivy League college;* or (3) *a sophisticated Continental.*[1]

The graduate of the Ivy League college can be, and usually is, a successful business man. And the man who dresses in the Continental style can be a graduate of an Ivy League college. But for our designation in this chapter these are the categories we will refer to, in spite of an obvious cross-over.

Clothes in any of the three wardrobes can reflect good taste or poor taste, can be handsome or cheap-looking, can be reasonably priced or outlandishly expensive.

I have selected public figures from the last 10 years to illustrate each type of dresser. Harry Truman wears clothes favored by the successful business man. John F. Kennedy wore clothes preferred by many men who have gone to school in the Eastern part of the United States. Cary Grant wears clothes that reflect a Continental's preferences.

If you feel comfortable in clothes worn by the successful busi-

---

1 Often referred to as *"the padded look," "the natural look,"* and *"the fitted look."*

ness man, your well-tailored clothes will have a certain weighty, substantial look whether you are wearing a business suit (double or single breasted), a casual jacket (tweed), or a sweater (cardigan.)

If you wear clothes favored by Ivy League graduates, your clothes move easily with your body, are natural-looking, not padded, your lapels are thin, and your trousers are narrower than those worn by young men in the middle west. You wear a narrow tie and your look can be described as "conservative." You feel comfortable in a blazer when you go in for sports—and the sport you like best is sailing.

As an older version of this man, your clothes will have the same narrow look, narrow lapels, narrow, easy fitting trousers, narrow ties. You will wear barrel cuffs, not French cuffs with cuff links.

If you prefer the Continental look, you prefer less conservative clothes. And your taste ranges round the world. You may have a raincoat from England, a tailored suit from London, good sports coats in subtle greens and browns, and your clothes have a fitted look.

If you are still wondering which of the three types you tend to resemble, answer the following:

Say, you are off to a football game with a group of men whose opinion you respect. In which of the following will you be considered well dressed by your associates? (1) A business suit and a camel's hair coat? (2) Flannel slacks and a tweed jacket? (3) Continental slacks without a belt with a houndstooth black and white checked jacket?

(Number one is the football look of the successful business man. Number two is the football garb of Ivy League. Number three is the football look of the Continental.)

Such a test is not truly indicative, because all types will at times wear clothes favored by the other two. But we do tend to be comfortable in a certain type of clothes which has nothing to do with physical comfort. This psychological comfort is the result of our background and rub-off from our associates. (We tend to dress as the people we spend time with dress.)

The first rule for being well dressed is to *feel* well dressed. You will feel well dressed if you remain true to the type (explained above) which best expresses you.

As you read the rest of the section, keep in mind the one in three types you most resemble. All bargains mentioned can be obtained in all categories of clothes.

Finding a model

If you are unsure about what clothes are right for you, make a mental note of a man in your city or state or in the news who looks every day as you would like to look. For a short time, as you shop, consider what *he* wears. When you are buying casual shoes, for instance, consider whether he would wear loafers or sneakers or short suede boots. Notice how he folds an ascot, if he wears one. Does he wear a vest? A colored one? What color? At home in front of the fire, would he wear a smoking jacket, do you imagine, a cashmere sweater or a madras jacket? Notice what hat he wears to church when you see him there—a homburg, a derby, or a conventional felt?

This may be child's play to you, and if so, skip it. But the best-dressed man I know told me that when he was fresh out of college he selected clothes that he knew the best-dressed man in his town would approve of.

"I gradually began to absorb his taste as I mentally tried on *him* everything I considered buying," he told me. And then, he added, "I even managed to get the name of his tailor."

If the man whose dress you admire has a tailor and you know who that tailor is, begin going to him yourself. Naturally, you are not going to copy the man's suits. You are simply going to assure yourself of the same good fit and tailoring details.

Right now you are probably objecting. "Tailor? Who's got a tailor? I don't have a tailor and I'm not about to get one. I can't afford it."

Now we're in for an argument. Because if you are to dress the way you want to dress, you should be able to call on a good tailor when you want to for several reasons. (1) You need at least one *pattern* suit that suits you exactly and *fits* everywhere—in the sleeves, shoulders, seat, trouser length, every way. If you never have another made-up suit, this *perfect* suit can serve as a benchmark for the selection of suits, jackets, slacks, vests—which you can buy off the rack. (2) You need a tailor to alter your suits and other clothes if you should gain or lose weight, or order clothes and find they don't quite fit. (3) You need a tailor who will measure you for clothes when you want to send your exact measurements overseas.

Suppose you want, now, to get the name of a tailor from someone in your town? If you are new in town you can simply ask, "Say, where's a good tailor around here?" If you are out looking for a good tailor for the first time in a town you have grown up in, you may prefer to be less direct. The main thing is to find the name of a good tailor who makes up the kind of suits you prefer. Now you are on the way to being well dressed. You know *how* you want to look; you know a man who exemplifies this look in your opinion; and you have the name of the tailor who keeps him looking the way you want to look.

So what is holding you back from being faultlessly tailored every minute of the day? The answer is one thing, *money!*

Dressing for less

You are lucky if you are an average-sized man—or if you do not have some flaw that prevents you from buying off the rack. I happen to have freakishly long arms. Whether I am buying shirts, jackets, sweaters, anything, I have to allow for this off-balance measurement. I have made enough noise about this, though, that everybody in the family who buys anything at all for me remembers to request "extra long arms."

By now this flaw in my physique works for me. It seems to be a challenge to people in the family who buy gifts for me. One of our daughters bought a shirt for me one time, only to find later that the sleeves looked like sleeves on a scarecrow. Since then, every year, she has sent to Hong Kong (Ascot Chang, 34 Kimberly Road, Lowloon, Hong Kong, BCC) for a custom-made shirt for me. Jean gives her an old shirt of mine that fits perfectly to send along with her order. When we started this book, she told me that she pays about $3.00 for a cotton shirt, and it fits perfectly, long arms and all.

> TIP: *Call attention to members of your family to any flaw you may have. The gifts you receive will be all the better for this.*

Because of our way of life, casual clothes are of more interest to me than are the other types of clothes. But I still have to have in my closet a good dress suit which I need for occasional events. I don't intend to replace this even if the lapels on the suits of my friends may narrow or widen a little in the next few years. My closet holds three custom-made business suits, a classic style bowler (derby) which I bought from Lock & Company at 6 St. James Street, in London, for $13, and a black silk suit which I had made in Rome the first time we visited Europe a few years ago for $90. (For this suit, a good one, I went to Lineo next door to the American Express at Via Due Macelli 60. If you want the tailor recommended by world-traveler, Temple Fielding, as the king above kings, go to Brioni to have a suit made at Via Barberini 79, in Rome. You will pay $135 for a suit made by the tailor who made up clothes for the late President Kennedy when he was in Europe.

Duty on a custom made silk suit if you send for one or bring it home is 37% (figured on the retail price), or, on a wool suit, 21%.[2] Suits not classified as custom-made are figured on the wholesale price. I have a Burberry trenchcoat with a detachable lining in my closet which will last for years. I bought the coat for $50 in

---

[2] I paid no duty on the Italian silk suit I had made. I wore it in, declaring it with my $200 worth of duty-free goods I was then allowed. Other high duty items I declared with my duty-free allotment. Lower duty items we paid duty on.

Burberrys, Ltd., 18 Haymarket, in London. I've got a couple of good madras jackets. (One is an orange striped job which I bought for $14 in Bermuda probably because timid shoppers were afraid to buy it. The same jacket here, if I could find it, would be $45 and nobody would be afraid to buy it. I receive more compliments when I wear this than for any jacket I have ever owned.) I've got two cashmere cardigan sweaters and a grey wool slipover that one of the children brought from W. Bill, Ltd., in London, that will be favorites of mine years from now. I've got an Irish knit hat that I bought half as a gag at a stopover at Shannon Airport for $4.50 last year and wear here on misty days. I've got a buckskin shirt I bought in Minneapolis with a 10% off coupon I found in the "See Minneapolis" book handed to me at the Sheraton Ritz. The saving I do by buying at the source gives me an over-all mark-down of far more than 30%. I've got things in my closet I like now and will continue to like for years. Each of the things I have mentioned, you will notice, is a classic in its own right.

RULE TO FOLLOW: *When you travel, buy articles of clothing that will not go out of style. You not only can get classics for less when you buy at the source, you will enjoy these good buys every time you put one on.*

My feet are as normal as my arms are abnormal, so I send for shoes on occasion and do fine. I have sent in the past year, just as an experiment, for British Shoes for Gentlemen as advertised in the *Saturday Review* (loafers, $10.95, including tax and duty); rugged service boots for $14.50 through the mail order house of Knapp Shoes [3] through a catalogue I picked up at the Danbury Fair. (The ones I got are calf high, made of natural reverse leather with no laces and have a pacifate lining and waterproof soles.)

I don't aim for a best dressed list, but the clothes I wear suit my needs well. And many of the things I own and like (such as

---

[3] Knapp Shoes, Brockton, Massachusetts.

the London trenchcoat) are regulation items in the closet of America's best dressed. Yet, I think little about clothes, and spend far less than others in my same economic bracket. Not just 30% less—*but far less!*

For that reason you may be interested in the simple rules I use as a guide for buying clothes.

1. Have one suit expertly tailored at least every two years. (This year my one major investment is a Cambridge grey business suit with natural shoulders.)

2. Know the outstanding bargain house near your own home. (Example: In Norwalk, Connecticut, an hour away from us, there is a factory outlet store at the American Hat Corporation, a company that makes hats for Knox, Dobbs and Cavanaugh. This store, which in the beginning sold hats alone, now sells all kinds of clothing at discount prices. Typical buy—English tweed topcoat, imported by Knox for their Park Avenue Shop—discounted because it was an "irregular"—price, $32.)

3. Don't be afraid of mail order. It saves time and money—offers a chance to get exceptional merchandise, otherwise not available. As I said, I order shoes and boots by mail, get more than 30% off. My wife orders my shorts and undershirts by mail (she orders plain colors—you pay more for fancy prints which I don't favor, anyway). She orders black knee socks in stretch fabric for me, a dozen pairs at a time. (I match them up when they wear out one at a time.)

4. Buy at the source. I got a sheepskin coat (*vrai mouton*) for $55 at the Flea Market in Paris. I brought it home with my duty free allotment. A few days ago, I saw the same style coat (but not in the same olive beige color tone) at a local department store for $195. I have to make myself buy when traveling, because when I am spending money for an expensive trip, I am inclined to hold back on buying. This I know is a

false economy. Clothes bought at the source are the best buys a man can get. And, of course, the opportunity to buy at the same good source may not come soon again.

5. I buy for use—and select clothes to wear for whatever I'm doing each day in line with what I bought it for originally. (I wear short sleeved polo shirts, cotton or jersey, when I'm working outside in warm weather. In the winter, I wear long sleeved wool shirts, when I'm working outdoors.)

6. I make it a point to look at details of workmanship wherever I'm buying. I look for machine stitching in clothes I'm going to be giving hard wear (it outwears handwork). And I have learned how to detect hand workmanship in clothes when I'm buying too. At the Gentlemen's Resale Shop, 425 Madison Avenue, New York, where I've taken our boys to look for good buys in jackets (samples or jackets worn on TV shows), I can spot handwork in a few seconds. (Test: Crush the lapel of a coat or suit. If it springs back into shape it shows hand workmanship. Such outer signs indicate that there will probably be hand stitching inside the coat where it counts.)

7. I buy classics—in everything—shoes, boots, jackets, raincoats, eyeglasses, wallets, sweaters, ties, *everything*. This assures 60% more wear for everything I own. Like most men I never get tired of the things I like.

If you are an average man, you probably do not think about your clothes much until you have to have a suit or a coat or a pair of shoes. Then, you may buy with little relationship to the rest of your wardrobe or even to your regular needs. Changing your buying habits takes some thought. But once you make the switch and begin buying according to an overall plan to suit your particular needs you will *feel better* in the clothes you wear and at the same time you will *save 30% or more* on everything you buy.

5

Clothes for Women

by Jean Kinney

It is my belief (and Cle's too), that the money a woman spends on clothes is a good investment for her and her family. You may not be spending enough, but don't cut. Spend what you are now spending, but get *three times as much for your money.*

How to be one of your town's best dressed

1. Look to Paris for the inspiration for at least 80% of your clothes.
2. Find a mill end shop for fine fabrics.
3. If you do not sew, find a talented dressmaker.
4. Join committees that run Thrift Shops and rummage sales.
5. Find bargain stores that buy up leftover merchandise from top American designers.
6. Understand the reason for every sale you go to.
7. Invoice your wardrobe, selling everything you never wear.
8. Put all hats, gloves, bags, jewelry, lingerie that you never wear in a large box. Trade these for something.
9. Buy regularly from one shop and from one salesperson.

Paris

Twice a year Paris produces a city full of glittering showcases filled with suits and coats and dresses which are studied and copied by merchants around the world, and twice a year the

Fashion Group in New York (consisting of 2500 women engaged in the business of fashion or an allied field) brings over Paris originals for a one day show for members and their guests. Originals flown directly from Paris come from Capucci, Pierre Cardin, Castillo, Courreges, Dior, Ferreras, Givenchy, Nina Ricci, St. Laurent, Simonetta et Fabiani, and Venet. Originals *purchased in Paris* were lent for the last show by Alexander's, B. Altman, The Arkins, Bergdorf Goodman, Hattie Carnegie, Celanese, Davidow, Seymour Fox, Harry Frechtel, Frank Gallant, Kimberly Knitwear, Harold Levine, Lord & Taylor, Macy's, New York, I Magnin, Montgomery Ward, Ohrbach's Originals, Suzy Perette, Ben Reig, Abe Schrader, Jerry Silverman, Hannah Troy, and Zelinka Matlick.

American merchants adapt or copy Paris things for their own sales of "copies of Couture Imports."

The last time copies of Paris imports were offered by Ohrbach's, *thousands* of American women *and men* stormed the store. One man carried home suitboxes filled with clothes totalling more than $2,000. (He bought line for line copies, in the original fabric, embroidered in the original yards, for far more than 30% off the Paris price.) Copies are not as high as originals, but even so, an exact copy of a St. Laurent navy wool dress with pleated skirt, white pique necklace, sold for $169.99.

A pretty steep price for the wife of a man making $10,000 a year, but a bargain over what you pay in Paris. At a haute couture house a suit costs about $500 and an evening coat may run to $1,000. American department stores and manufacturers who buy with the express purpose of copying pay *four times* or even more than that price. They pay for the privilege of using the original as a pattern.

Paris originals are translated by the great American houses and then translated again by cheaper houses. A Chanel suit may be created in Paris and sold to Princess Stanislas Radziwill for $800. Nine months later something vaguely like it will be sold to a girl in Illinois for $79.50. To understand the merchandising of a Chanel suit, let's take a good look at the most copied designer who ever lived.

Coco Chanel

Diana Vreeland, editor-in-chief of Vogue says that in the late Twenties there was one dressmaker who understood what the postwar world would mean to women. Coco Chanel. "She understood 40 years ago that we want to be comfortable, clean, easily kept up—everybody making an appearance every day. Her understated suits (for which she is most famous) are uncrushable and move as you move." Chanel herself says about her slim easy clothes with the rich-poor look, "In my dresses, you can get into a car any way you want."

According to Naomi Barry, author of the best guide book to Paris (in my opinion) ever written, *Paris Personal,* "Chanel loves to be copied." She once told Naomi "I remember a night 35 years ago when I went into Ciro's and saw exactly 26 Chanels and Chanel copies dining there." And she went on, "I couldn't figure out which ones were mine, but I found the whole effect very pretty." Sophisticated Parisiennes make a game of trying to *separate the copies from the Chanel originals* at top restaurants.

According to Francoise de Langlade, an editor at Paris Vogue, Chanel has a way of working the fabric which actually lightens it. Francoise swears that material worked by Chanel is three times lighter by the time it ends up in a perfectly-proportioned suit than it was before she started her fitting. And to quote Naomi Barry again "A Chanel sleeve is a marvel of engineering. It is as spare as a sheath, yet if you wanted to you could wear it and pitch a baseball. The jackets hang as well open as closed. The skirt is a matter of balance, in motion and at ease. When Mlle. Chanel prepares her models, she may adjust a jacket a dozen times, altering it by a millimeter here and there until imperceptibly the ideal is reached."

Chanel's "little nothing" suits are as right for a woman of 50 as they are for her daughters. The fabric that goes into each one costs $25 to $30 a yard, every button is handmade. But the genius comes from Coco herself, who stitches endurability and elegance into every line of a suit that can go to a dental appointment in

Kansas City as rightly as it can go to "21" for lunch. Jane Fonda wears Chanel suits, Jean Seberg wears them, Princess Paola of Belgium wears them.

For women less rich, there are copies, and copies, and copies. According to Europe's Hebe Dorsey of the Herald Tribune, out of 100 suits sold at the semi-couture houses on the Left Bank in Paris, 75 are Chanel copies.

In order to buy a Chanel suit (either an original or a copy) you've got to be able to recognize one. Go to your local library, search through the periodical index until you find a picture of a Chanel suit. You will see a little, usually collarless jacket, shorter than usual, pockets, a suit of soft wool or worsted or tweed (nubby) lined with silk. The skirt will be slim, sometimes slit to reveal its lining of matching silk. The blouse will be in the same silk, usually sleeveless, no bulk, no doo-dads. Make up your mind now to make a suit like this your first purchase in your streamlined wardrobe.

If your husband is one of the wealthy ones, buy an original

Now that's a funny statement to find in a 30% off book, but think about it, and you will find that the advice makes sense. Coco Chanel is in her 80's—her classic suits are works of art. You will be just as right in one five years from now as you will be in a cashmere sweater. Besides, you can change the look without changing the feel by having your Chanel suit dyed when you're tired of the color.

(*Example:* Vogue's Francoise de Langlade bought an original Chanel four years ago in red. This year she took off the buttons, had it dyed dark blue. Chanel's button woman refused to sell to anyone except Chanel, so Francoise went to the house of Chanel at 31 Rue Cambon and picked up buttons ordered by Chanel, herself. Today, Francoise has a Chanel suit, as easy-hanging now as the day she bought it, in a new vivid color, with buttons by the little button-maker. She has already cut the cost of her original investment 50%—and four years from now she can dye the suit purple and get some more buttons.)

But suppose you don't have $800 for that original suit, what then? You can go to Ohrbach's or Macy's in New York, or to another large city store and get line-for-line copies in the original fabric. You pay about $295 for a Chanel copy at Bergdorf Goodman, New York, long considered the best place in America to buy a Chanel suit, and there the fabric and cut and buttons are as close in quality to the original as it's possible to get. Ohrbach's prices for Chanel copies are lower and the fabric and workmanship are excellent. It is occasionally possible to buy a good copy for less than a hundred dollars.

In *Europe on Five Dollars A Day*, Arthur Frommer tells about his wife's going to the Galeries Lafayettes in Paris and picking up a Chanel-type grey woolen suit for 100 francs ($25). Encouraged by that bit of news, I made my way there to the third floor. I didn't find any $25 models, but I did find three Chanel copies (identical classics in soft plaid tweed, pink plaid, blue plaid and cocoa) at a little more than $80 each. With my discount for American travelers' checks (20% French sales tax is not charged when you pay with checks bought in America) I bought a blue plaid copy complete with a hand-made silk blouse for $64. The silk is good, the fabric is crushable, details are almost unbelievable for the price (silk-cuffed pockets, four of them, blue and gold buttons, eight of them—silk lined skirt). I'll be wearing the suit for years. And back in America, I have had the *copy* copied, in better fabric than I bought at the Galeries Lafayettes.

Find a mill end shop or remnant place

Near Bloomingdale's on 59th Street in New York, there is a small one room Mill Ends shop. Each morning owner L. Barnhardt heads for 7th Avenue, calling on manufacturers like Maurice Rentner, Adele Simpson, Harvey Berin. "I ask to buy odds and ends of fabric—they give me 10 yards of Spinner silk they've no use for, or some yellow linen they bought for something they won't be making up after all, or some popcorn tweed in pink and white, maybe." He sells these ends for about one-fifth the price of soft goods at neighboring department stores.

You can't always get exactly what you go after at a mill ends shop. For my copy of the Chanel suit, I wanted black worsted, ended up instead with a navy worsted with a pencil-thin pinstripe in red, and pink silk for the blouse and jacket lining. Material purchased: 3 yards of navy worsted in 54 inch width—$3.95 a yard; 4½ yards of Slipper silk—about the same price. Total cost of material about $35. My dressmaker duplicated the suit for $45. Chanel suit—$80. Sophisticates can tell my copy from an original, but few can tell it from a Bergdorf copy.

Find a little dressmaker if you can't sew yourself

Get a dressmaker who can copy your favorite dress in a new fabric that looks as expensive, but not exactly like the original. Certainly you can find one who can sew from a pattern. Any dressmaker worth her weight in lambswool (the better to back up a hem with, my dear) can make a high fashion dress from a $3.50 Vogue designer-pattern and $40 worth of material ($28 dollars worth if you're thinking right) that out-ranks any on-the-rack $80 dress you can find in your local department store. (Vogue designer-pattern series gives you a choice of 50 or more styles by 18 designers like Dior.) Handwork [1] in a copy of a Paris couture dress is what costs a merchant money. Get a seamstress to do this handwork at home and you come off at least 50% better.

Second hand clothes

The last time I helped out as a marker at a thrift shop I saw in the boutique a black pencil shift from Cardin, with a narrow vee in the back descending down, down, down (some nice New York matron got scared to wear it), with a price tag of $45. At an

---

[1] Dressmaker details—Loops inside the shoulders of your dress for the straps of your slip; an inner belt at your waistline; zippers put in by hand.

auction of hats at a recent charity ball, I saw a yellow ostrich plume hat from Lanvin, worn once, sold on the block for $25. At a resale shop in Connecticut I saw a wonderful brown suit with a beautiful print stole by the American designer, Jablow, marked at $15. (Some woman must have gained weight to give that one up.) Last week one of the markers at the Nearly New Shop went home with a purple wool Hattie Carnegie dress for $12. I recommend Thrift Shops, especially those supported by charities which have wealthy members. The more sophisticated you are about designers and fabrics and dressmaker details, the better able you will be to spot a bargain at a church sale, thrift shop or resale shop.

Other suggestions

Subscribe to Vogue Magazine. Vogue interprets "the world of the Beautiful People." Subscribe! If you think the subscription is too high, get two other Beautiful People to get a subscription with you—then pass each copy around. Here is the best picture reporting from Paris in the United States today. Read and your taste will improve. You will come to know how a point of cut, color, or fabric sets one dress out from the crowd.

Study the Paris reports that come out in the spring and fall. All the clothes you see for the next year will be inspired by these fashions.

Read Eugenia Sheppard's column syndicated by the New York World Journal Tribune. This is the most readable fashion column in America. Read it whenever you can and you will automatically come to know more about clothes. Your skirt length will be right, your sleeve length will be right, your gloves, your bag—everything about you will look and feel smart.

Pay attention to well dressed women. As you look at a Johnny Carson show or the Emmy Show or the Academy Awards show, or at any TV show where women know they are being looked at, pay special attention to what they have on. When you see a picture of Jackie Kennedy in the paper, notice what she is wearing. (Except for being omitted in deference to her mourning, she is always on the Best Dressed list.)

Trade up. Read magazines which picture the homes of people who live at a level a step above your economic plateau. Soon your home will begin to have a flavor of far more expensive homes. The homes pictured in the magazine may have a half dozen chaise lounges; yours may have only one. But the chaise in your bedroom can be upholstered in the same fabric and good color as one you see pictured. And you can relax on it in hostess pajamas and an overskirt by Dior, made by your seamstress from a Vogue pattern.

Buy at the top houses. If you go to Paris (and 48% of American tourists do go there) make it a point to come home with at least one original. Also, make a point of getting it at 50% or 70% off the haute couture price. Buy at a clearance sale from a Dior, Lanvin, or any of the other great houses in the two week period just before new collections are shown. (I bought a yellow original coat from Nina Ricci at 20 Rue des Capucines for $65. It had been made by Crahay, no longer with this house. I also *splurged* on a Crahay dress at a "sale" price of $195 minus 20% for travelers' checks. Since that time I have had the dress copied, line-for-line in two different fabrics. I wear the original and my copies with equal pride.)

Many Americans are afraid to go to elegant shops in Europe or here. Go to the best! The owner wants you, is concerned now that you are afraid to come. And how can you know a bargain unless you know what prices are normally? Get to know one sales person well. Once she knows your likes and price bracket, she will call you with news of good buys.

Go to bargain houses

Bargain Houses for Millionaires, as they're advertised in New York, are as interesting as thrift shops, but built on a different principle. Dresses and coats in these shops are not donated. They are purchased by the store's owner, much as mill end fabrics are purchased, and are sold at a profit. They usually have not been worn, although occasionally a dozen dresses from a TV show spectacular may be offered for sale.

Once you understand clothes and you also understand merchandising principles, you will do handsomely in any bargain store. Look for these shops in Los Angeles, Chicago, New York. There are bargain shops in Paris that specialize in selling originals which may be left in the big houses after the clearance sales. Odd sizes, worn by very tall or very small models, are the ones with the greatly reduced prices.

Buy from your friends. The two best-dressed women I know are: (1) The sister-in-law of the president of a famous insurance company. (Every six months she gets a box containing good suits, cocktail dresses, an evening gown which her brother's wife is now replacing.) (2) The sister of a woman who owns a dress shop. (The merchant sister knows it isn't good business to wear the same cocktail dress time after time at the country club. So she sends her clothes to her sister after a few wearings.)

Ask such a person if you can *buy* the clothes she will not wear again. (She may be afraid she'll offend you if she gives you her clothes.)

Pay attention to sales. The best buys you will get at the top fashion stores will be at clearance sales, in late summer for summer things, in the spring for winter things. The better the shop, the better the sale, because no good shop wants to put tried-on clothes away for long months of storage.

Occasionally a department in a store is discontinued. (An elegant boutique may give way to a teen-age shop.) Then you can get great buys. Embroidered blouses, beaded collars, elegant, unusual things go for very little.

Buy glittery clothes, holiday ball gowns, fancy cocktail dresses at January sales. Get good buys in hats right after Easter.

HATS. Millinery has the biggest mark-up of any item of clothing for women. And the sales on hats have the biggest mark-downs. Rule for buying hats—*get a shape that's becoming to you!* Then have the hat duplicated by a milliner if there's a good one near you. Or search out a local milliner (like Lehrer's Millinery Shop at 1 West 47th Street in New York which sells every hat in the store for $5.95) which specializes in good hats at one low price. A place called Unger's at 42 W. 58th St., New York City sells sample hats from shows of hat designers in the metropolitan area. Like many sample hats shops in the 58th Street area, prices are much lower than "originals." Hats start there at $15.95. Let's hope your town has a good milliner, and that you are a good customer. In that case, you can take back last year's hat and have a bow or feather put on this year.

GLOVES. Order by mail from Italy, Bermuda or France. Consult Elizabeth Squire's "The Mail Order Shopping Guide" and other mail order lists. From Oberon, 73 Champs Elysees, Paris, you can get soft lined gloves for $5.90 that cost almost twice that here.

SHOES. Get comfortable ones for every day. I like Red Cross Shoes, which I order by mail, once having found my size, from Treadeasy Red Cross Shoes, Danbury, Connecticut. There I can buy an A heel and a D front, which I can't find in many shoes. By far the best buys in shoes I have ever found are offered by Tilkins, a manufacturer's distributor on Main Street in Charlestown, Massachusetts (a suburb of Boston). The most beautiful women's shoes made in the United States are offered at 40% to 60% off the price you pay in regular retail shoe stores. The reason is that in this store manufacturers can get rid of extra cuttings they have made for a fine shoe store. The Boston store does not compete with retailers in its own area—sells only shoes sold in big shoe stores far enough away to be unaffected by price cuts. No charges, no exchanges, no C.O.D.'s, no refunds, but if you're ever around Bunker Hill monument, go there. The shoes are sensational and cost $12.50 to $15.00 and even less at markdown sales.

Here's a tip for buying rubber boots. When new, put a quarter in each heel—the heel of your shoe won't puncture it, and you won't have to replace your boots next year.

LINGERIE. A girdle is comfortable as long as it feels firm. Find one that will not sag after a few washings. Send your correct measurements, if you order by mail. (Don't cheat. A girdle that is too small creeps up.) When buying a bra, *check the band under the arm.* If this band has no "give" your pectoral muscle will be constricted. Constant constriction contributes to sagging breasts.

With both your girdle and bra, support is your main consideration. With your slip, prettiness is the thing to look for. And, of course, it should hang right because it serves as a lining for your dress.

STOCKINGS. Buy by the dozen, getting a 13th pair free. All the same size and color so you can match up odd stockings.

BAGS. Buy lined bags made of fine, soft leather. Order from Italy, France or Mexico, or go to a handbag shop like John Suarez, 366 Fifth Avenue, New York City. He takes little mark-up, sells in volume, and pays little overhead. (You walk upstairs but save 30% at least on every bag.)

CLEANING BILLS. The biggest saving that has come to American women (and men) in the past few years is via coin operated cleaning machines. For 8 quarters you can clean ten pounds of clothes. If you are timid about popping in your best Paris suit, get over this. Your suit gets exactly the same treatment here that it does when you pay $8 or $10 for the same job.

BEAUTY CARE. Save 70% by going to a beauty school for services. (Shampoo and Set will be $1.50, when average price is $5.) Worried? Remember, the girl about to graduate will be getting $5 for the same work next week. Or find a former operator now married. She may come to your home. (I have such a gal. She charges 50% less than a shop and saves my going out.)

6

Dependents of All Ages
(The Care and Feeding)

Changing Times, published for consumers by the Kiplinger Magazine, Editor's Park, Maryland ($6.00 per year) sponsors a show on WNHC, New Haven. Last night their reporter told this story.

A man was contributing $850 a year to his 75-year-old mother's support. (The rest of her income was coming from Social Security.)

The woman spent $150 a year for medical expenses. The man could deduct her support, $600 a year, from his income tax. "Now," said the reporter on TV, "suppose this man paid only $700 toward his mother's support, and he paid the $150 in medical expenses. Now he still can deduct the $600 for her support, but in addition, he can deduct the $150 he pays out in medical expenses. (After 65, the 3% in non-deductible medical expenses does not apply.)"

There are many simple money saving principles to follow as you care for your dependents. (1) Your mate, (2) all your children under 18 years of age, (3) your children in college, (4) older dependents or invalids.

What about tax deductions?

1. *Your Mate.* Whether or not your wife (or husband) is working, file a joint return. (*For the whole year* even if you had a Christmas wedding.)

2. *Your Children.* For every child you support under 18 years of age, take a $600 exemption. (Even for the new baby which arrived on New Year's Eve.)

3. *College Students.* Take $600 for each child you are sending to college, even if that student earned more than $600 this year. If he earned less than $600, he should file a return. Then he can obtain a refund for any tax his employer may have withheld.

The Bureau of Census statistics prove that a male college graduate will earn $175,000 more during his productive lifetime than will a male high school graduate. So get your child to college.

Consult your local school or public library for a list of available scholarships to colleges in your part of the United States. Do this when your son or daughter is in an early high school year; then work *toward* a scholarship.

One way to finance a college education is to apply (through the college of your choice) for a loan under the National Defense Education Act Student Loan Program. A student may borrow $1,000 per year up to a total of $5,000 starting with his freshman year. No interest is charged while the student is in college, but after graduation he pays 3% interest and can take up to 10 years to pay back the loan. This is an especially good plan if your child wants to be a teacher: then, 50% of the loan and interest can be forgiven at the rate of 10% for each year of public school teaching.

A new opportunity for a free college education came in 1965 to boys who could qualify to participate in the Army ROTC vitalization program. Any boy who qualifies and agrees to serve as a commissioned Army officer for four years after graduation from a participating college or university can get his tuition, textbooks, room and board plus $50 a month in spending money as he goes to school. (He can take any work he wants to take, but he must take part in ROTC.) By 1970, the Army expects a participation of 5500 undergraduates in this program. The Navy ROTC has a similar program. If your son is interested, consult the school nearest you with an ROTC program for further details.

Many states—Connecticut, Indiana, Massachusetts, New Jersey,

New York, North Dakota, Rhode Island, Virginia and Wyoming, have loan programs for students. Many colleges give low interest (1% to 4%) to students with repayment starting after graduation. Many religious and business organizations have loan programs for students. If you are paying for your child's education but want to spread out payments, finance through one of these plans: The Tuition Plan, Inc., 18 School Street, Concord, New Hampshire; The Insured Tuition Plan, Inc., 6 St. James Ave., Boston 16, Massachusetts; or the Investment in Education Plan, Funds for Education, 319 Lincoln Street, Manchester, New Hampshire. No need has to be proved for these plans which include an allowance for good living in a sorority and fraternity house and an insurance policy on your life in case you die before repayment.

4. *Your Payments for an Invalid Member of the Family.* You can deduct $600 for this dependent if you contribute more than $600 support, even though that person may be collecting Social Security retirement or disability benefits. (Talk with your local Social Security office. Compensations here are often overlooked.)

Best break any member of our family ever got in Social Security payments was a dentist who reached the age of 72 at almost exactly the same time that Social Security for dentists went into effect. He paid one Social Security payment; then, became eligible —has been collecting a monthly retirement benefit every month since. And he still works in his office full time. (Note: After you reach 72, you can earn any amount and still get maximum payments.)

Pre-school children

Here are expenses you will have: (1) food, (2) a doctor, (3) clothing, (4) a nursery school (optional), (5) a baby-sitter or other help.

Prepare as many foods as possible yourself. Prepared foods cost more. (Some instant foods cost 50% more than foods you start from scratch.) Mash your child's own potatoes and bananas, and make your own applesauce. Use dry skimmed milk whenever possible, rather than whole milk. As soon as possible, offer a variety of foods, not expensive foods, but different. You will have less trouble later on getting your child to eat what the rest of the family eats.

During pregnancy, get a doctor and follow that doctor's advice exactly. If your regular doctor has a long, good record of delivering many babies, you will save money if you do not employ an obstetrician as well as your regular doctor. If you live near a good clinic, save money by taking your baby there for checkups and shots rather than to a pediatrician. Check your local hospital to see if there is a baby clinic there and if you are eligible (sometimes there are economic restrictions). You want your baby to have required shots for polio, diphtheria, typhoid and everything else. Whether they are given by a nurse at a free clinic or by a pediatrician in an expensive office, the shots are the same.

About clothes: Dress your children well, but not "way out." Children are self-conscious. The French have the most attractive children's clothes in the world. The Cadeau Volant, 12 rue de la Ville-Neuve, Paris 2, France, puts out a catalogue twice a year that sells for $1. Send for it—you can get a feeling of children's fashions even if you do not buy dresses through the catalogue.

For everyday clothes, get simple clothes (so the child can dress himself). Don't let your child wear clothes that are too big, expecting him to grow into them. Your child should *feel right* in his clothes. Hand down clothes if you like, and get clothes at a resale shop if they are attractive, but don't make your child wallow in big clothes—or squeeze into small clothes.

Know the difference between water-repellent and waterproof clothes. (Water-repellent refers to the finish, alone; waterproof garments have both fibers and cloth coated with chemicals.)

Buy playclothes at Penney's, Sear's, Ward's, and W. T. Grant's. Look for sturdy linings, flat, secure buttons, seams that won't come out. Baby clothes should have flat seams for comfort. Disposable diapers are fine if you are traveling, but not for every day. They add to expense as do prepared foods. Buy shoes of flexible leather that are roomy at top as well as the sides. Don't hand down shoes (that can cause foot trouble later on)! If you have several children, buy new shoes in standard sizes at special sales. Children outgrow shoes in about three months; if a boy has standard size feet and you know anything about fitting shoes, someplace along the line the shoes will be the right fit for him.

About entertainment: Avoid highly merchandised wind-up toys. Provide bicycles and sleds and dolls (with no tricky mechanics to go wrong), skates, all the old standbys. Provide creative playthings.

What about a playschool? In New York City, some of the playschools are as expensive as junior colleges in other parts of the country. In other cities, well publicized schools often run by universities or colleges have a waiting list *years* long.

If your child is denied playschool privileges because you can't afford an "ultra" school, talk to the Head Start [1] people or form a recreation program with the help of other mothers.

In New York a group of mothers formed a Neighborhood Recreation Committee at 885 Columbus Avenue for youngsters two to five years old. After appealing to the Children's Aid Society and the Health Department, they won a "go-ahead" to start the play group (first registration brought in 50 families). Mothers run the entire operation from the setting up of equipment to teaching (done by 12 trained volunteers), supervising play, dispensing refreshments, and talking over family concerns. Anyone in the neighborhood can join by paying 25 cents. Children are divided into age groups and meet on Tuesday, Wednesday, and Thursday, from 9:30 to 11:30 A.M.

"We set the 25 cent fee deliberately so that everyone taking part would do so on an equal basis," the group chairman said.

Such a program gives mothers a break in routine and helps them to know other mothers. With the help of the city's Department of Parks, the group moves outdoors in the summer.

Form a mothers' club. (Let one mother take the children

---

[1] Call your local school board to see if your town has a Head Start program. If your family income is $3500 or less, your pre-school children are eligible.

skating, another give them drawing lessons, another read children's classics, etc.) Start a night-time baby-sitting group. (Each mother can give "hours" of baby-sitting time to members of the group in return for "hours" when she needs help.)

School children

In these years, children should be well fed and well dressed, not expensively but comfortably and in fashion. Sources are the same as they are for babies—and sales logic is the same as it is for you.

For the entertainment of these children, create a mothers' car pool. (I'll take the children on Monday—you take them on Tuesday, etc.) But pool your creative talents, too. The mother with Little Theatre work can organize a children's theatre. Every mother can help, but the experienced mother can direct. Children whose mothers work together in a common project will have security that others whose parents pay but do not participate can never know.

Other dependents

If you have an older person living with you, give that person quarters of his or her own. Spend the $600 you deduct for his support to put in a small range and refrigerator in a room next to his room—or get a construction mortgage and build a small apartment in your home and pay it off at the rate of $600 a year. The dependent will feel independent and you will not feel put upon.

If your dependent is a woman, this is even more important. Psychologists say that 90% of all differences between women who have to live in the same home occur in the areas of cooking and child care.

Let every dependent contribute

The happiest family we know has a widowed aunt living in her own "suite" on the first floor.

"Aunty" is busy at her desk and at the telephone all day long. She is family secretary.

When the family wanted a puppy, she found a free one through the A.S.P.C.A., 441 East 92nd Street, New York (TR 6-7000). He was inoculated free, too. "Aunty" got a free plan from the light and power company for turning the back shed into a green house. Now the family has an herb garden. She called attention one day to a sale at the grocer's of avocados. "If you hear the loose seed bump around when you shake it, it's ripe," she told the children.

"Aunty" found a wallpaper shop on Route 7 (Ronals, New Milford, Conn.) which buys leftover rolls from manufacturers anywhere. "A manufacturer uses a certain color of ink every time he runs off a pattern," she told the man of the house. "The exact shade is never the same in another run, so they sell the leftover rolls to Ronals. You can buy wallpaper there for $1.50 a roll that sells for $5.40 in New York."

At Christmas-time, this busy secretary sent one of the children to the five and ten for styrofoam balls, plus tiny beads and spangles. Total investment $4.00—and Christmas balls with the spangles pinned on them were the delight of the women who received these ornaments as gifts. For the men on her list she gave blue and white striped woven-denim aprons (with a halter at the neck and a tie at the back) worn by English butchers in the Smithfield market in London. She ordered them from General Trading Company, 144 Sloan Street, Sloan Square, London, S.W.L. "Only paid $1.90 for them, but they're very chic," she whispered to me.

If you want your dependents to be happy, help them to be independent. Send to the World Journal Tribune for "65 Ways of Finding More Fun in Retirement." Enclose a stamped, self-addressed envelope and 10 cents to cover handling costs.

7

Medicine and Dentistry

Two emotions keep medical and dental bills high in some families. One is *fear,* the other is *guilt.* A parent with a sick child becomes frightened. A person with an unexplained sick feeling becomes frightened. In either case, he goes to a doctor for relief of *fear.* A parent whose child is sick may feel guilty that he has not done right by this child. A person whose parent becomes ill may have the same guilt feelings. With fear or guilt in his emotional make-up, he will pay more all along the way—for medicines, for calls on the doctor, for a nursing home, for hospitalization, for everything connected with his medical problems. He actually asks to be overcharged.

Warns one consumer magazine: "The only real safeguard against being overcharged for medical services or anything else is the wariness of the consumer, himself." Be wary!

Knowledge takes away fear

The more you know about your own physical make-up and the makeup of your children, the better equipped you will be to care for them. Take a course in first aid. (Your local Red Cross office will either offer such a course or will tell you where to find one.) Take a course in Family Care at the YWCA. Get a "First Aid Textbook" from your local chapter of Red Cross for 75 cents. And send for free books, like the ones on the next page.

Preparing for Parenthood	Metropolitan Life Insurance Co.
Your Baby	1 Madison Avenue
Understanding Your Young Child	New York, N.Y.
Nine to Twelve	
Understanding Your Teenager	
Booklets on Childhood Diseases, Alcoholism, Cancer, Heart Disease	
When Our Parents Get Old	
List of Booklets Available on Senior Citizens	Public Affairs Committee Inc. 381 Park Avenue South New York 16, New York

A well-stocked medicine chest will have very few items in it. Inexpensive aspirin, sodium bicarbonate to combat simple indigestion, a milk laxative like milk of magnesia, rubbing alcohol to be used as an antiseptic, toothpaste (or soda if you really want to save money), adhesive bandages, and tweezers for taking out splinters. Do not stock your medicine chest with highly promoted laxatives, ointments, and oral cleansers.

Prevent big hospital expenses by covering yourself and other members of your family not eligible for Medicare with health and accident insurance. Investigate your coverage before your need for it comes up. More than 6,000,000 Americans have health insurance policies that will pay in part for nursing home care. Many do not know this. Check to see if you have coverage when you are making a decision about a nursing home for a member of the family. Remember, too, that through Medicare any senior citizen in your home is eligible for 20 free days in a nursing home after a hospital stay—80 more at $5 a day.

Check your insurance policies to see that the wage earner in your family has coverage for lost earnings due to absenteeism due to illness. Know what benefits are now available to older dependents in your home.

Buying with a group will lower your insurance premiums; paying annual premiums rather than in monthly payments will bring down the cost of insurance. Add health and accident insurance payments to your annual medical expenses. (If medical expenses are 3% of your income, such expenses are tax deductible.)

Dealing with your doctor and dentist

The "ethical" demeanor of doctors and dentists prevents some persons from talking price. Do not put off this kind of discussion, especially when you are contemplating a large-scale dental plan. (We know a woman who had her "bite" changed, and in shopping around for the best price for a bridge to raise her "bite" got prices ranging from $395 to more than $1000.) If you are considering orthodontia for a child, discuss braces with several dentists. When you find the dentist you want, offer him a price just as you offer a contractor a price. Tell him that your child will come at odd hours, will cooperate to fit in with his schedule. But tell him exactly what you can afford. You may not get a lower price this way, but if your dentist is just beginning to build a practice you will get a good reception. Certainly, you can select the best orthodontist you can find for the price you want to pay.

If you live where there is a dental college, go to the university clinic. Serious students may be even more conscientious than old-time dentists.

Talking to several doctors about a proposed plan is more difficult. Usually, by the time you go, you are too ill to shop around. The best thing is to settle through the years on a general doctor for whom you have respect.

When you check into a hospital, let hospital authorities know what insurance policies you have and make it understood that you want your coverage to come as close to total coverage as possible. Carry the numbers of your policies with you at all times.

Some policies cover psychiatric care. Use these benefits (especially after a traumatic accident which has put you in a hospital). By reworking your mental attitude, you can speed your recovery.

8

Transportation

Are you more interested in *where* you are going or *how* you are going? In the first frame of mind, travel expediently, and in the second, travel in style.

(Examples: When we cruised the Caribbean, we were not interested so much in the half day we would spend in Barbados, although we planned what we would do there, as we were in enjoying the cruise itself. We planned for comfort in our stateroom and a good table in the dining room, and booked passage on a line that insured the kind of daily living we prefer. When New York photographer Jim Bates and his wife took off for Spain, they went tourist on an old German ship. Once in Europe, they bought a Vespa and went over the Alps and camped out in Spain to get the pictures they wanted. They sought inexpensive transportation every mile of the way.)

What is the purpose of your next trip? Relaxation? Or do you want to get to Italy, say, as fast as possible to do a book or study art or the language? Then, save money on the trip and spend it in Europe.

Think of your car in the same way. Want one to get you where you have to go? To school with the children, downtown to shop, to the station with your husband? You need a sturdy non-gas-eating compact. Or do you like to take long drives up into New Hampshire "to see the color"; weekend trips to places like Rockport for a look at the sea; a drive to Atlantic City to see whether the old place has changed? You want to *cruise*. Get the most comfortable riding car you can buy.

On a business trip to Europe, go by air. And go tourist. (Most companies insist on this substantial savings on employee travel now.) If you are going for a long, leisurely vacation, go over by air and come home by boat. To travel as inexpensively as possible, go by freighter or go tourist on a boat, or go on a plane chartered by a group.

Specials

A travel agent quoted these prices to us today for a trip to Texas. Round-trip from New York to Dallas, for one person—first class, jet $192.40 (tax $9.60); same round trip for one person, tourist, $166.40 ($8.32 tax); or about 13% in savings. For two persons, the first class fare of $404.00, as compared to the tourist class of $349.44 makes for a saving of $54.56 on the trip. Now—we learned from our agent—that if we go Braniff any time from 6 a.m. on Monday until 6 a.m. on Friday, or on American from 12 Noon Monday until 6 a.m. Friday, we can go "family plan." This means the husband, in a man and wife pair, will pay full fare of $166.40 (plus tax); the wife will pay 75% or $124.80 (plus tax). Now we have two figures that spell out a lot of savings—$404.00 if we go first class on Sunday; as compared to $305.62 if we go tourist on Monday for a saving of $98.38. More than 20%. That's the way we will go for this trip.[1]

About *off season* rates. Pan Am advertises jet economy fares to Europe from the U.S.A., except from May 22nd to August 3rd; and from Europe to the U.S.A., except from July 17th to September 28th. In those periods, all fares go up $85 or more round trip. By coming to the U. S. on July 16th and returning September

---

[1] There is even a less expensive way to go. By propeller plane rather than jet. That way the fare is $144.80 per person plus $7.24 tax (with a family plan available). Now the overall savings go up to 30%. For our trip we would have to make five or six stops rather than go straight through, so we will go jet. But always ask about propeller flights.

29th, you save $85 over what you would spend if you came one day later and returned one day earlier.

When we accepted an advertising assignment to Europe last year, we were given two tourist plane tickets, TWA, to be used anytime within three months. One of us went over early, the other came for a 10-day period. At the Paris office we were booking passage back *for one* after the 10-day stay when the attendant said, "If you stay *four more days,* I can return you $110." We were amazed and delighted. Airlines to Europe offer excursion rates for trips of from 14 to 21 days. The purchaser of our tickets bought regular fare tickets. We received a *cash refund* when we switched to excursion rate. Make sure you take advantage of excursion rates. You travel in the same manner that you travel when you don't go excursion.

(Question of ethics: In the example above, should the company which purchased the tickets get the refund when such a refund is made? Or does this belong to the individual? In this case, the refund belonged to us, because the tickets which we accepted were given to us outright as part of the deal. Employees of a company whose expenses are paid not on assignment, but day-to-day, are expected to return such refunds.)

When traveling by train, ask about round-trip fares. If you are going a short distance and coming back the same day, you sometimes can get more than 40% off; come back the same weekend and you get a big reduction too. Especially promoted trips are always good buys. Big savings reported by friends of ours was on a trip sponsored by Railroad Enthusiasts, which went from Albany, New York, to Rutland, Vermont, and returned via the Delaware & Hudson, a Boston & Maine freight line and several branches of the old Rutland Railroad. There was an open gondola car for good picture taking, a dining car and coaches. Fare was $8.50 excursion rate for adults, $5 for children. Contact E. J. Rollins, Box 258, Caldwell, N.J. if you want to join the group. Membership fee, $6 a year.

Go tourist on a plane and save. The drop is even greater on a ship. "Queens" fares from Cherbourg to New York on the Cunard line drop from a first class fare of $451 to $279 for Cabin Class to $216.50 for Tourist Class. More than 50% from first class to Tourist! And be sure to ask about excursion fares if you are going both ways by boat. There you can get an even greater price cut, a 25% cut in addition to the Tourist Class reduction.

Your car—is it better to own or to rent?

In a large city, you can save money by renting. The average N.Y. City motorist drives about 7,000 miles a year. To clock this mileage, we learned recently, they use their cars about 300 hours a year, leaving them idle about 95 percent of the time.

The New York car owner pays about $200 a year for car insurance, $18 for his vehicle registration, $325 for gasoline, oil, tires and maintenance, and about $500 for a garage. This amounts to more than $1,000 . . . and we have not yet figured in depreciation.

The disadvantage to renting is that at the end of a year, you have no equity in the car for the money you spend with Hertz Corporation, Avis, Inc., National Car Rental Systems, or Kinney Service Corporation. But if you drive a car 100 days a year to clock the 7,000 miles your cost is $1,700, only a little more than the annual cost of *maintaining* your own automobile.

We recommend renting in a large city for three reasons. (1) You have less cash outlay for the same amount of driving; (2) you have less fuss; (3) you don't do nearly as much driving. Renting a car occasionally is an event.

Figure it this way. For what you pay for a garage for a car, you can take two 85 cent cab rides a day in New York. Another thing, in New York, you probably will take those two cab rides even if you keep a car.

Outside of New York, to figure whether you should lease a car from a rental company with a full maintenance lease for $130 a month or buy your own car, you will have to compute costs of ownership—depreciation, insurance, gasoline, oil, maintenance, garaging, registration and taxes. If your car is idle 90 percent or more of the time, you will do better renting.

Wherever you rent, check the rental concerns that offer budget rates—Budget-Rent-A-Car in New York, Econo-Car International, Ltd., Alexander's, and others. Rates range from $5 to $8 a day for compacts; major rental concerns charge an average of $10 and 10 cents a mile for 24 hour days. (Like the airways, some not-so-busy days of the week have a lower rate, $7 instead of $10.)

In New York, you can rent a standard-size deluxe sedan for $5 and 11 cents a mile if you use it only between 4:15 P.M. and 9:15 A.M. the next morning.

Renting can save you money and *energy*. (Example: One New York advertising man comes in from Cincinnati at 11 at night, lands at Kennedy Air Field, and has to think about wending his way home to Darien. He takes a cab into New York, takes a train from 125th Street, takes a cab from the station to his home in Darien, gets up in the morning, drives his car to the station, parks it there and takes a train to his office in New York. The other man takes a rented car from the airport home to Darien, drives it into New York the next morning. The renter spends less and travels easily, the other *pants.*)

On a trip in a foreign country, take your car, rent a car, or buy a car. In Europe, with your own car, consult British United Air Ferries, Victoria 4479, in London. You can fly with your car to places you would like to see. (Example: Fly it from London to the Black Forest and the heart of Switzerland—and to the Riviera, Italy, and Austria. The service is not cheap, but convenient, and low rates prevail from the 27th of September to the next July 1st.)

Without your own car, several concerns in Europe make it easy for you to buy, rent or lease a car. Besides Cars Overseas at 10 Rue Pergolese, Paris, 16, there is Auto Europe with offices in Frankfurt, London, and Paris; and there is Auto-xport, Inc., 141 Broadway, New York 6, N.Y., which will ship you an *American-made* automobile at a New York price for use in Europe. (Delivered at any port you say.)

Or buy in Europe, use it traveling, and bring it home at a low duty as a used car. If you want to get a Peugeot when you arrive in France, write or talk to Cars Overseas, 555 Fifth Avenue, New York 17, N.Y., before going on your trip. You can buy a Renault in Europe through Car-Tours-In-Europe, Inc., 2 East 46th Street, New York 17, N.Y. (Comparative prices: Dauphine Sedan in United States $1595; in Europe $1147.) Car Tours in Europe tells us they recommend renting a car in Europe if your trip there will be for less than 15 days; leasing a car for a flat agreed upon sum if your trip will be more than 20 days; buying a car and bringing it home if your trip is for more than 20 days and you need a car in the United States; buying a car and reselling it yourself if your trip is for more than 30 days and you don't need a car at home.

Rentals are arranged as they are here; leasing is different. You get a new car, registered in your name, fully insured. You agree to pay a flat charge for unlimited use of this car for a specified period. (Example: When you rent a luxury car like a Mercedes-Benz in Europe for two months, you pay a rental of $920; lease and you pay $545.)

When driving in Europe, select a small car to keep gasoline costs down. (Angry Frenchmen insist that with their high gasoline taxes, every automobile driver in France makes a gift of an automobile to the state every three years!)

The French Railroads have a service for car owners. You can take a trip and have your car brought along on the same train in the car behind your compartment on an excursion rate. (Just 10% in addition to your tickets, for your car. And tickets for family excursions often are reduced 75%. As a tourist inducement a European in America can travel for less than Americans can travel; Americans can benefit the same way in Europe.)

Daily transportation

Here are five price-cutting approaches.

1. Share expenses with two others, instead of driving alone, and you save far more than 30%.

2. Instead of taking a cab to work, take a bus. In New York City, you can cut transportation costs this way 90% or more.
3. Buy bus tickets, by the dozen or the book rather than a single passage. Same with tokens in most cities. (The only city we ever heard of that has a first class and a second class *on a subway*, is Paris, on the Metro. Go second class! On a subway, who cares?)
4. Consider gas consumption as you drive. Do three errands per trip instead of one (there goes 66% off right there).
5. Drive an *uncomplicated* car, one without lots of gadgets to go wrong. Check your gas consumption. Get rid of a gas eater.

Summing up

In public transportation you can save money if:

1. You book long trips for off times.
2. You take advantage of family fares, excursion rates, and multiple ride prices.
3. You charter a plane or a boat or a bus with a group.

In private transportation follow the RIG theory of keeping costs down.

Repairs!
Initial Cost!
Gas Consumption!

The lower the RIG, the better the car is for *you!*

9

Getting Away From It All

On our cruise to the Caribbean, a young singer (whom we never heard of before or since), made two appearances and got her trip *free*. The recreation director who planned the bridge tournament, the children's race, and the masquerade ball got her trip free. The dancers got pay plus travel. The American Express man who handled island tours got his trip as part of his job. The ship photographer got a commission for each photograph as well as the trip. If you have a talent, even a little one, you can get away from it all *for nothing!*

A European management consultant told us that in his 20's he traveled free seven times from Europe to the United States as a ship photographer. This was no Irving Penn or Alfred Eisenstaedt. But he *was* a natural salesman. (Passengers on ships do not expect a *Bachrach portrait,* they just want to take home pictures of themselves in costumes or at the captain's cocktail party.) Our European friend took pictures he knew would sell.

On a ship, these people go free: seamen, officers, stewards, shopkeepers on board, American Express people, entertainers, directors of entertainment for passengers and their assistants. Apply to the purser of a ship. When traveling, services are as good an exchange as money.

Have you lived in the Scandinavian countries, or in Greece, or in Israel? Do you know Russia, Egypt, or Australia? Travel agencies need persons well-versed in the ways of a country to conduct tours. Are you a teacher, a former counsellor?

A tour conductor goes with 15 persons (if the fares add up substantially) or with 25 persons (if the fares add up to a lesser sum). You can get free transportation from a large agency if you sell 12 persons the idea of taking a tour. Some agencies charge full fare to all going in a group but help a tour director collect his expenses from others in the group. (Example: Seven students from Canterbury Boys' School and an instructor toured Europe. The instructor, who collected one-seventh of his expenses from the parents of each of the boys, rented a car in Europe, booked hotel space, arranged the itinerary, and gave lessons about each country enroute.)

Going with a group

Your expenses are less when you travel as a member of a railroad excursion club, a hiking club, a jeep mountain climbing club, or on a plane with a club, than when you travel alone. Handle the details and you can travel for nothing.

Charter flights have the same equipment and are as well staffed as regular commercial flights. So encourage your club to charter a plane to Europe. Offer to handle all arrangements in exchange for your trip. But keep in mind that "affinity regulations" of international airlines permit you to charter a plane only "on behalf of members of a group which has objectives other than travel." You can't form a club just to get a reduced price. And you can't let someone join to go along. Members must have belonged for six months before flying.

To get a charter, your club will have to guarantee a rental of around $30,000 for a trip from the United States to London and back. Can you encourage club members to take 64 pairs of tickets at $260 a ticket, round trip? If so:

1. Find out if your club is eligible. Ask the Traffic Department of an overseas airline for information about charter flights. Ask for a choice of dates (within a period of six or eight weeks), and for the cost of a charter for a 130 passenger jet.

2. Make sure that the reaction of your club is enthusiastic.

3. Now, tell your president that you will handle all business, publicity, promotion, and bookkeeping for the trip, in exchange for a free trip for you and your husband or friend. (Expenses are spread out among all ticket buyers and added to their fares. So is a donation for your club's favorite charity.)

4. To clinch the sale, tell your president that you will pay full fare if the club's quota is not reached. Only if you go over the necessary number of sales will you go free. (Even if you should have to pay, you still will be going to Europe for much less than regular fare; this remains true of charters even at this time when fares to Europe are becoming less expensive all the time.)

For small clubs, airlines now make it possible to charter as few as 25 seats on a *regular* flight. Group fares purchased this way are more expensive than tickets on charter flights, but are less than regular fare.

Enjoying your trip

Charter flights are the fastest, cheapest, and easiest way to travel. Once you get overseas, you do not have to spend time with your group until you re-group to come home, usually one month later. If your club has promoted the trip through a good airlines or travel agency, you will be royally treated. If you want to rest, paint or write on your vacation, get on a freighter, but allow as long as 14 days to cross the Atlantic. (Many freighters leave Norfolk, Virginia, which carry passengers as well as freight, and charge as little as $130 for passage to a European port. And there are Yugoslavian freighters that leave from New York, stop at Tangiers, where you can cross over to Spain, for as little as $120 for the one-way passage. If freighter travel interests you, send $2 to Glaessel Shipping Corporation, 44 Whitehall Street, New York 4, N.Y., and subscribe to the monthly Glaessel Newsletter of Freighter Sailings. You can book a berth three or four months ahead of time. Don't believe that you won't know your destination ahead of time. You will!)

See the world

"Join the Armed Forces and see the world" is n̥ ke. Many men (and their families) like military life because t̥ ̥an travel around the world this way. Or they join the Peace C̥ ̥. In 1961, young people were assigned by the Corps to constru̥ ve tasks in underdeveloped nations. Soon, it became apparer̥ that older people were equally (or more) suitable for some v̥ ̥k. Now the Peace Corps is open to *all* persons, of any age o̥ ̥ if they have no dependents.

At the last report, hundreds of Peace Corps members (now numbering 7000 but estimated to go as high as 18,000) were over 50 years of age. And the Peace Corps would like to recruit several hundred additional retired persons—particularly those with college degrees and skills.

If you want to work for the Peace Corps, whatever your age, fill out an application blank at your post office. If your qualifications make you valuable in some part of the world, you will be called to take a 1½ hour exam at your post office. What your references say about you will be highly important, as they are on any job application. If you are selected to go overseas, you will be sent to a university for 12 weeks of indoctrination and then will embark on a two-year assignment. You can state where you prefer to go but you may not always get the assignment you want. Your transportation and a living allowance will be given to you. (This living allowance will permit you to live in the same manner as natives of the country where you are going to live, who do the same kind of work you will be doing.) You will also receive a salary of $100 a month, $75 of which is banked for you in the United States and will be saved for you until you come home.

The government pays your way home even if you have to come home (due to forces beyond your control) before your two years time is up.

Right now more than a million Americans are seeing Europe as Europeans by working abroad. *For information about government positions* overseas, write to the U. S. Civil Service Commission, Washington 25, D.C. And at your post office you can get *Form 57*, the standard application for Government employment; also, get *Form 5000-AB*, which is an application to take the Federal Service Entrance Examination.

The Air Force, the Army, and the Navy all maintain overseas employment offices in Washington. All Government Departments (Commerce, Interior, State, Labor, and Agriculture) send specialists and clerical people overseas. The U. S. Information Agency, 1776 Pennsylvania Avenue, N.W., Washington, D.C., which operates the Voice of America radio network, has many career opportunities around the world plus openings for clerical workers, librarians, and administrators. The Central Intelligence Agency has a free pamphlet, *Employment Opportunities in the C.I.A.*, at their Office of Personnel, 2430 E Street, N.W., Washington 25, D.C.

Ask your post office about America's International Development Program. A.I.D. secretaries earn about $4,500 annually, get free transportation and housing.

Send for *Guide to Employment Abroad* published by Hill International Publications, P.O. Box 79, East Islip, New York. The cost is $1, postpaid.

This lists jobs in non-profit organizations such as YMCA and USO, positions for nurses, jobs for secretaries and good opportunities for librarians, teaching positions in out of the way places, jobs with construction companies and many managerial positions that are open. Employment opportunities in transportation companies, newspaper and press services, employment agencies, social work, and jobs for great American companies like Gulf Oil, Remington Rand, and General Electric are listed. Summer jobs in work camps are included. (If you are primarily interested in teaching, order "Teaching Opportunities Overseas" from the above company. The price is $1, postpaid.)

If you are a teacher

The latest issue of *Crusade for Education,* published by The Advancement Placement Institute, 169 North Ninth Street, Brooklyn 11, New York, lists teaching opportunities in schools, colleges, museums, and universities in Canada, Ethiopia, Lebanon, Turkey, Australia, Borneo, England, Ghana, Greece, Guatemala, Jamaica, Japan, New Zealand, Nigeria, Nyasaland, Sierra Leone, and Switzerland.

If you have a particular place in mind where you would like to live and teach overseas (Hawaii, Norway, Peru, anywhere) send to Applications Services at the Brooklyn address above for a guide that will tell you what positions are available at that particular place. (The cost for a specific guide for one country is $1.)

If you are a student

If your school has an exchange program with students in European colleges, or if it has a program whereby you can study for one semester in a foreign country, take advantage of this. You pay no more that you do to attend school where you are going now; even transportation is furnished in some instances.

For graduate work, consider going overseas. The pamphlet, *Education,* which you can obtain free from the Superintendent of Documents, Washington, D.C., 2040, lists information centers for higher education in Argentina, Bolivia, the Philippines, and many other far-away places.

Renting with friends

Take a house somewhere like Mexico for a year, and sell off the rent to eight couples, with each one's taking a summer and winter vacation. Houses are also available in Puerto Rico, Hawaii, Jamaica, and in all the resorts. In Central America, too, where the American tourist spends less on a vacation trip (average expenditure $285) than he does in any other vacation place (average $577).

To get information about houses in any country, write to the Tourist Bureau of that country. (Example: Mexican Government Tourist Dept., Paseo de la Refroma 35, Mexico City.)

Cheapest vacations of all

If you are a walker, you have all kinds of vacation possibilities open to you. Most large papers, for instance, print a column of weekend hikes organized by such groups as the American Youth Hostels, or a college alumni hiking club or a local group called by a name like the Ramblers. Hikes are divided into categories of easy, moderate and strenuous. Search out these groups wherever you are, if you like to walk.

People to people

The People to People organization, located at 2401 Grand Avenue, Kansas City, Missouri, works for round-the-world friendship, and has as its chairman General Dwight D. Eisenhower.

This organization encourages ice skaters to get in touch with other ice skaters in all parts of the world, chess players to get in touch with other chess players, artists to get in touch with other artists, etc. It will put you in touch with tourist bureaus, hotel associations, and development commissions that will help you to meet others interested in what you are interested in.

Money-saving tips

1. Arrange transportation on a long trip with a group, even though you do not stay with the group for all your travels.
2. When renting a vacation place, rent for the season with several couples, or rent for the year and sell off weeks to other families.

3. Buy a boat at the end of the season—or from a man who is dragging his feet to clean his boat up for the season.

4. Ask about excursion rates; rearrange your time to take advantage.

5. Camp out. (Some countries encourage camping out. In British Columbia the Government maintains sites with barbecues for cooking. Free firewood is provided. Sites are free the first two nights; after that a fee of $2 a night is assessed.)

6. Go to countries or states holding out inducements to tourists.

7. Go through a travel agency when you are going the conventional way. The service costs you nothing. (The agency gets a percentage from the hotel or transportation it books.)

8. Don't tip when a service charge (10% to 20%) is added automatically to your hotel bill.

9. Do your own room service. Take in your own fruit, snacks, instant coffee. Room service costs for merchandise plus tips.

10. Let your job pay as much of your vacation as possible. (Let your wife, or husband, meet you on your business trip near a vacation place.)

11. Do your homework before leaving home. Send for free maps, brochures, and side trips.

12. Until (or after) you give your every thought to a full-time career, take any work that gets you around the world. Join the Peace Corps or one of the armed services, or work on a ship or in a travel agency. (After you have worked a year in a travel agency, you get 75% off on all your hotel and transportation bills, wherever you go.)

10

Gifts

We collect Christmas gifts all year long and wrap and mail them the weekend after Thanksgiving. We love this weekend because it is a reminder of the places we've traveled during the year.

In one drawer or closet we put gift items. Along with them we put favors, small prizes we win, bargains we find at antique shops and auctions, and even things we *no longer use.*

(The most unusual gift we ever received was a group of Georg Jensen silver napkin rings, given to us by an advertising woman who had just lost her job. "I am not spending money for gifts for friends this year," she told us. "Instead, I am giving things of my own which I have always loved." We love those napkin rings!)

Keep a permanent storage place for gifts!

The business man who goes to a foreign country has a unique opportunity. He travels for nothing so he can bring in his allotted gifts duty-free on a ticket that someone else provides. If he gives gifts to his children purchased the week before Christmas at a United States department store, he is missing something. His wife can help him by packing into his brief case a sheet listing native products and what he can expect to pay for them in the country where he will be visiting. If he reads this on the plane going over, he can arrange an hour or two off to pick up some things near his hotel or the offices where he is doing business. With his eyes open for these purchases, he will see other products she never even heard of![1] And his Christmas gifts will be glamorous!

More conventional business trips

Not every business man has a chance to pick up a camel ($45) in Libya, but many men west of the Hudson go to New York once or twice a year, and often these men take their wives along. Here is a chance for wives to shop for items for the gift closet, but often these wives don't know where to look for unusual gifts in Manhattan. How can you pick up beautiful handbags at marked-down prices from Fine & Klein's Handbag Shop, if you don't know about this shop, or know that it is located at 131 Orchard, all the way downtown? And how can you, when you're down that way, get ropes of seed beads from Haiti in a great choice of colors at $1 per rope, if you don't know that Phyllis sells them at her shop at 175 West 4th Street in New York? And how can you pick up a designer dress for your daughter at a reduced price if you don't know someone who carries them like Jeanne Macdonald in an office building at 55 West 42nd Street? And you can't snip a snip from your daughter's hair and take it to New York when you go and have a lovely wig made as a surprise for her, if you don't know that you can get one reasonably priced at Edith's Beauty Salon at 17 West 57th Street.

Our suggestion is that before you go on any trip you begin a file of bargain items. Then you can plan an afternoon in one section of the city you are visiting. (Example: If you have an hour leftover from shopping in the 50's in New York, you may stop in at the Lighthouse Craftshop and pick up a long wool skirt handsomely knit by one of the blind, at 111 East 59th Street; then go on down to the New York Exchange for Women's Work at 541 Madison Avenue near 55th Street for a look at the handcrafts on

---

[1] He can have a suit custom made for his daughter in Hong Kong, but for surprisingly little he can also have a rug handwoven for his wife by three or four women, each one of whom weaves in a different color, in a pattern just for him.

the second floor, antiques on the fourth floor. Here you can find embroidered sweaters for little girls in your family, at a good price. Most of the work is made by consignors. Tea is served from 2:30 to 5:00 P.M. Cinnamon toast is a specialty. A pleasant hour in New York that you can't possibly plan without knowing where they are.)

Most hotels give you a "Guide to the City." Map out a buying plan. This way you can get all the things done you want to get done, and you can pick up gifts that you can't buy at home.

Number one rule for buying away from home: *Buy something you can't get at home!*

We have a rule for favors we take to friends. We keep a shopping bag with us for small (not junk) take-home presents, and we get all-of-a-kind items whenever we see a real bargain. In Capri one day, we found unusual rings set with large polished native stones. They were less than $1 a piece, and we bought 10, in all shapes and sizes. We gave them to the teen-agers we know who collect costume jewelry. We bought cameos this way in Naples, limoges perfume atomizers this way in Paris, silk ties for men in Rome, and pipes in London. As friends and relatives greeted us back in New York after this trip, we gave each one a small gift from our take home bag which we had brought back from somewhere in Europe. Rather than search through Europe for exactly the right gift for Kristy or Jay or Damon or Carmel or Jo or John, we bought quantities of gifts of a kind, one group for teen-agers, another for male adults, etc. It took no more than an hour's total time in all our travel time in Europe to get take-home gifts for everyone.

Gifts for our Christmas gift closet we select differently, although we put Capri rings and cameos from Naples and pipes from England in there, too, if some are left after we have given gifts to friends whom we wanted to remember at homecoming. Never, and we mean *never,* do we start around a new city (when on a trip) by saying to each other, "Here is where we pick up a Christmas gift for Uncle Cliff," or for somebody else. Instead, we

buy unusual gifts for many different age groups—and because we
have a large family which takes in all ages—every gift we select
can be given to one of five or ten persons. We do watch each
other, however, to keep ourselves from buying more than we need
for little girls, for teen-agers, or for any one particular group. We
usually come out fine. And if gifts of a category are left in our
gift closet after Christmas, we don't worry about this. We give
them to persons in that category for birthdays the following year.

This kind of mass buying gives us a chance to pick up many
bargains at one shop or in one mailing. Last year Henri Bendel's
ran an ad for monogrammed towels for children (a bath towel,
face towel and wash cloth, with the name of the child monogrammed free). We sent for five sets of towels with the name of a
different grandchild monogrammed on each one. As a birthday
has come up this year, we have reached into the box from Bendel's
and sent off a towel set. By now, this advance mass buying seems
to us the *only* way to shop.

Obviously, we do not fill our Christmas boxes with unusual gifts
from Italy if the only trip we have taken all year has been to the
Autumn Pilgrimage in Virginia. (The year we did that every
family on our list got a ham delivered Christmas week, sent direct
from Smithfield. And the young architect on our list got a brochure which we got free from the Virginia Department of Economic Development, 811 State Office Building, Richmond, pic-
turing the great Virginia houses shown at Pilgrimage time.)

The year we happened to be in Paris at sale time at the couture
house, we came home with glamour gifts for all the women on our
list. By poking around at sales of left-over items from last year's
collection (next to the perfume drenched ballroom-size salons
getting ready for the new collection) we found remarkable bargains at Pierre Cardin (118 Fauborg Saint-Honore), Carven (6
Rond-Point des Champs-Elysees), Christian Dior (30 Avenue
George V), Gres (1 Rue de la Paix), Jacques Griffe (5 Rue
Royale), Lanvin (22 Rue de Faubourg St. Honore), Jean Patou
(7 Rue St. Florentin) and Nina Ricci (20 Rue des Capucines).
We found some white ermine slippers (ridiculously frivolous but

loved by the daughter we gave them to) at Lanvin's for $3 and *a dress at Dior for $2.* The Dior dress was a freak, and even the sales girl could not believe the price tag. It was a very tiny size (even for a dress worn by a French mannequin) and had hung on a hanger through two seasons.

Let your gift-buying tie in with the life you lead. At the Danbury Fair we noticed some handmade woven wastebaskets, simple and well made, for 97 cents each. We bought six and put them in our gift closet. We will tie a great red bow on the handle of each next Christmas. In each one we will pack gifts for families we deliver to *by hand.* An inexpensive but clean-lined wastebasket will look pretty elegant, we think, if we leave it all beribboned on the doorstep of a young couple and have it filled to the brim with such things as sandals from Rome, a leather covered lighter (which we picked up for 50 cents at a Little Switzerland Shop in Saint Thomas); a bottle of *creme de menthe* from France and an apothecary jar filled with thyme. The whole Christmas package will cost no more than $7, wrappings and all, and nothing other than the herbs and waste basket will have been purchased this year. (The lighter we bought in a lot of a dozen in the Virgin Islands several years ago; the sandals ditto in Rome two years ago; *creme de menthe* we bought in France; the apothecary jar we bought with a dozen jars for $10 at an auction. We filled the jar with thyme which anyone can order by mail from the free catalogue of Pharmacie Francaise, 581 Tenth Avenue, New York 38, N.Y.)

We buy at auctions just as we buy in foreign countries. We may go to buy a hutch for the kitchen, but at the same time we look for groups of objects. (Small crystal perfume bottles, maybe six carved mahogany masks from Africa, or a collection of miniature antique furniture. This last we found at an auction one August, which is the best time in a large city to buy at an auction. A lot of people are away then and competition is reduced. Merchandise goes cheaper than when the season is in full swing.) Often, at an auction, the auctioneer sells many little, not too valuable objects as one item, rather than slow up the sale. Such groups go cheap.

(the crystal objects we got for $6; the mahogany carved things for $9; the antique furniture, really exquisite, for $17.) We gave the furniture to a little girl in sets of rooms; and gave one big girl, a decorator friend, the French drawing room, which has become her pride and joy.

Most popular gifts

We find that the best received gifts we give are wall hangings. Therefore, we look for unusual wall hangings of all descriptions. For instance, in the basement of the Louvre, in the "Department of Chalcography," we bought engravings, pulled off 18th century copper plates, for $1.80 (if they are hand-colored after originals of the period, they sell for about $5 a piece). We also found Lautrec prints and excellent prints of paintings by Renoir, Braque, Matisse, Picasso, and Manet. We bought more than 20 in all and have given them one at a time in boxes we sent at gift times. (Be sure to check the information desk of any American museum you may be visiting and find where to buy prints and other objects. If you want to order prints from the Louvre, send 50 cents in stamps to the Department of Chalcography, Louvre Museum, Quai de Louvre, Paris, France, for a catalogue.)

At the Louvre we bought plaster reproductions of plaques (Medusa, reproduced from the bronze; a Greek God's head, reproduced from marble) both for less than $6, both equipped with hooks to hang easily on a wall. Both are handsome gifts.

Two museums in Philadelphia, the University Museum at 33rd and Spruce Street and the Philadelphia Museum of Art, sell reproductions of sculpture and primitive art owned by these museums. Many beautiful pieces, not offered anywhere else, are sold on the premises and through their catalogues.

The advantage of buying masks or plaques as wall hangings is that you do not have to frame them. We find that our friends love the prints we give them, but love them more when we have them matted and framed. For that reason, we give sculptured wall pieces to friends where framing may be a problem, give unframed prints to persons we know can mat and frame their own prints or will be glad to pay for framing when the print is good.

We seek unusual prints (no Mona Lisa), little known things, and *small*. We feel that it would be conceited of us to send a gift to take up a large space on a friend's or relative's wall. We cannot possibly match individual tastes this accurately. But we have found that small, unusual wall pieces or prints are received with real excitement. No apartment, no matter how small, is too small to accommodate a reproduction of a Byzantine Ivory plaque ($3.50 at the Walters Art Gallery in Baltimore) and no home is too grand to disdain a gay little Lautrec print (for a nook in the ground floor sun room off the informal terrace) straight from the Louvre.

Because we know that the framing of a print can be more expensive than the picture, we pick up frames at the Salvation Army and second hand stores and auctions, and keep them in our woodshed. Sometimes, when we want to be especially generous, we mat and frame a print in a suitable frame. (Example: From the Louvre, we brought home an 18th century French print of the celebration that took place at the time of the birth of the dauphin son of Marie Antoinette. This we framed in a border in the style of Louis XVI.) This kind of gift, of course, is more appreciated than any other, because it involves a gift of the giver's mind, his taste, and real work.

Our daughter saw in a gift shop a wall hanging with small figures appliqued on beige muslin, then framed as a picture. "I loved the effect of the different textures and colors working together on a neutral background," Gwen told us. She adapted the idea, gave us a silver axe appliqued on a chestnut colored background. It hangs in our kitchen.

An artist friend brought us a housewarming gift—a piece of chestnut on which is painted a strong and handsome hand of a man. The pointer finger points to our downstairs bath off the big kitchen. Vulgar? No, it is too handsome and functional to be vulgar. But it does bring a smile.

Unusual gifts which are not expensive

If you want to take a gourmet food to someone in Europe, take over a jar of peanut butter, some dry cereal, or some barbecue sauce. And you will be as much of a hit as will the native of Holland who brings you a nice ripe Gouda cheese. The things you take for granted may be a rarity in other places.

When buying in a foreign country, *buy where the natives buy.* Go to department store basements.

In France, we bought wooden handled butter knives and small bowls for butter for a total of less than 75 cents. The knife stands straight up in the butter packed in the bowl. We bought net shopping bags for 29 cents a piece. We brought back children's illustrated cook books (good way to learn to cook French food and learn French, too). Bring home cooking utensils, inexpensive bread servers, hand-decorated plates, unusual cosmetics, and pay what a native pays who buys on a modest salary. (Really you will pay less because if you buy with American travelers checks, you save that 20% or more in taxes.)

When you buy ski clothes or bathing suits abroad, buy where local women buy, not in the expensive hotel shops which cater to Americans. Buy soaps and bath powders and hair sprays which have a few words of a foreign language explaining what this object is for. In an inexpensive Paris variety store we bought containers labeled *Sels pour le Bain,—bath salts!* Made of plastic, they cost about 20 cents each. We brought them to the United States, bought large quantities of bath salts here, and gave the containers filled with salts as gifts. With the French words, easily understood because the use for the bottle is obvious, the bottles are fun for our friends, who keep them in the bathroom.

Bringing home gifts from far away places has been an American custom for years. Note this letter written in 1758 by Benjamin Franklin to his wife, Deborah, in which he told her the following consignment he was sending home from London shops.

China cups and bowls.

4 silver salt ladles (newest but ugliest fashion).

A little instrument to core apples.

Another to make little turnips out of great ones.

Six coarse diaper breakfast cloths.

A little basket, a present from Mrs. Stevenson to Sally, and a pair of garters to you, which were knit by the young lady, her daughter, who favored me with a pair of the same kind, the only ones I have been able to wear, as they need not be bound tight, the ridges in them preventing their slipping. Goody Smith may, if she please, make such for me hereafter. My love to her.

Carpeting "for the best room floor."

Two large fine Flanders bedticks.

Two pair of superfine blankets.

Two fine damask tablecloths and napkins.

56 yards of cotton, "printed curiously from copper plates."

7 yards of chair bottoms "printed in the same way, very neat."

("These were my fancy; but Mrs. Stevenson tells me I did wrong to buy both of the same color.")

7 yards of printed cotton, blue ground, "to make you a gown. I bought it by candlelight, and liked it then, but not so well afterwards. If you do not fancy it, send it as a present from me to sister Jenny."

A better gown for you, of flowered tissue, 16 yards, of Mrs. Stevenson's fancy, cost nine guineas.

Snuffers, snuffstand, and extinguisher. The "extinguisher is for spermaceti candles only and is of a new contrivance to preserve the snuff upon the candle." Some music Bill bought for his sister. Some pamphlets for Susy Wright.

A mahogany and a little shagreen box, with microscopes and other optical instruments loose are for Mr. Alison, if he likes them; if not, put them in my room till I return.

Two sets of books, a "present from me to Sally." *The World* and the *Conneisseur.*

7 pairs of silk blankets, very fine.

"You will excuse the soil on some of the folds; your neighbor Foster can get it off.

"1 beer jug with coffee cups in its belly, packed in the best crystal salt, of a peculiar nice flavor, for the table, not to be powdered."

Long before this book was ever thought about, Franklin was instinctively shopping the way we have learned to do. And, busy executives take note! Even when serving as the agent of Pennsylvania in England, Franklin had time to send home gifts and household supplies from the London shops.

How to save money and time when buying gifts that everyone will appreciate!

1. Keep a permanent gift place in your home or apartment.

2. Buy unusual small items in quantity for take-home gifts.

3. Do not buy individual gifts for particular persons. Stock your gift place with quantities of unusual items, then select gifts for individuals from your own warehouse.

4. Buy as you travel, finding out the specialties of the country before you arrive there.

5. Buy where the natives buy, not in tourist places.

6. Give small wallhangings.

7. Adapt creative ideas from others and make your own gifts.

8. Buy gifts long ahead of time.

9. Keep your gift place well stocked for birthdays and special days coming up for a year ahead.

Part Four

Let the Joneses
keep up with you

Don't Be Afraid
to Jump Off
the Merry-Go-Round

A friend of ours resigned as president of a junior college. "I left," he told us, "because I was spending so much time on administrative duties, I was losing sight of what I once had wanted to do." He is writing a book. "It may not be a great book," he told us, "but as I write I can decide what to do next."

A $65,000 a year executive left his job to go to Columbia for a graduate course in political science. "I had been too close to my job for too many years," he said. "I needed time away to clarify my thinking."

An advertising art director left his high-paying job in Minneapolis to move to a farm near Sauk Centre and paint. The president of a national organization surprised his associates by resigning to move to Germany, where he now is with the U. S. Consulate Service. "I am using all the skills I learned when I was working in a big organization," he wrote us, "and I am using mental muscles I haven't used for years." A mother of two school children hired a housekeeper and took a job in a local TV station. "The time I spend with my children is more profitable now than when I stayed home," she says.

Don't be afraid to jump!

We own a real estate business called *Possibilities Unlimited* in New Milford, Conn. Many New Yorkers come looking for the *retirement dream house* they hope to be living in *ten years from now*. We are always depressed after a visit from a policeman or a teacher or a tired-looking executive who is simply putting in time until he can retire. Ten years from now he may be dead. As Gauguin knew sixty or seventy years ago when he turned his back on a successful banking career to go to Tahiti to paint, *today is the day to begin a dream!*

Sometimes you are shoved into a dream. You may be fired from a job. Before scrambling for another, ask yourself, "Is this the work I want?" Illness may force you to change climate. What new opportunities will be available to you in your new home? A death in the family may make your old way of life impossible. As the old door closes, look for the new one to open. It always does.

A friend may push you. In 1929, cartoonist Woody Cowan went up to Connecticut to visit John Held, Jr. who took him to see a "great buy" in an old farm. Cowan was unimpressed, but his friend put $1,000 down on the farm for him and mailed him the bill. Today, when his farm is worth 12 times its original cost, Cowan thanks his good fortune for Held.

One of the most successful merchants in the middlewest told us that a big job offer pushed her into her own business. "In the early 1920s, Killian's Store in Cedar Rapids offered me $9,000 to come there as their buyer. That was a fortune in those days. I decided if hard-headed Al Killian thought I was worth that, I was worth even more to myself. I opened my own shop."

Don't make money your goal

Italian style-setter Pucci whose shirts and scarves and dresses are loved around the world, recently said, "Money is not the goal. If you do something good, money rolls into your lap. I measure my success by my leadership."

If you have a talent, use it. The money will come. If you have a job in which you are not using your talent, switch. It is easier than you think.

Some Money Is Free

From time to time you will be eligible to receive money that you do not work for. If this money makes you feel rich, take it. If it makes you feel poor, don't take it.

You feel rich when:

- you win a contest.

- you receive a scholarship or a grant which makes it possible to do further work.

- you receive word that an unknown uncle has left you a sum of money.

- you receive a check from the government for clearing your property in accordance with forestry instructions.

- you win money on a television show.

- you win money in a beauty pageant.

- you win at Bingo.

You feel poor when you accept a relief check. (The residents of Appalachia, the prime target for the United States war against poverty, want Federal aid, but resent being called *poor*. "We may not be rich, but we've got enough to eat and a place to sleep." A welfare worker said, "Our folks are proud.") Avoid relief, but take unemployment insurance. Or should you?

Unemployment insurance

If you should lose a job, whether you have been earning $4,000 or $40,000 a year, you are entitled to a maximum 26 weeks of insurance, if your employer has been taxed for employee compensation. Taking such compensation may be a reminder that you have been fired, and therefore, distasteful to you. But before you decide not to apply for insurance, know these facts.

The weekly check mailed to you is a benefit made possible through a tax which your employer pays. (The worker pays nothing.) When you apply for insurance your employer is charged for your claim. Your employer does not resent this charge unless this severance puts him into a higher tax bracket. Employers of many people pay the maximum tax now.

If you are at an age where you may never be able to work again in an insured job, take your compensation which will be $1300 if you receive the maximum. If you are in a high-priced job and off in search of another, forego the check. Your image may suffer if it is noised around that you are taking unemployment insurance, and, anyway, you will have to spend precious time registering and reporting to the state employment agency. You do not receive the check automatically. You must file a claim just as you file any insurance claim.

Some housewives and laborers manipulate their lives to get on a payroll just long enough to be eligible for unemployment insurance and then manage to be severed from the payroll. Then, they are eligible for unemployment. The effort hardly seems worth the reward.

Social Security Benefits

There is no stigma to the acceptance of Social Security benefits, because all who are eligible (employees, their employers, and self-employed people) pay taxes which go into special funds. When earnings stop, benefit payments are made from the funds to replace part of the earnings the family has lost.

If you have not checked what Social Security benefits you will be entitled to in case your earnings stop, talk to the Social Security administrator nearest you. (Look under U. S. Government, Education and Welfare Department, or call your local post office.) Before seeing the representative, get a record of all the income that the government has credited to you. For this statement, send your Social Security number to the Social Security Administration, Baltimore, 35, Maryland.

Money saved on taxes

Money returned at income tax time isn't free money, but like Blue Cross benefits, it feels free. Here are claims that you may not have been taking.

- Claim expenses of at least five cents a mile when you use your car for business or for charitable work or for trips to the hospital.
- Work three years overseas and you will get a sizeable tax deduction. Check with a good accountant before signing a contract.
- Rent your home during the summer and your home becomes a rental property. You can take depreciation.
- Tickets for theater benefits are deductible; other theater tickets are not.

Consult a Certified Public Accountant when you make out your income tax. He will save you more than his fee, which averages about $75.

Dividends and interest

Columnist Phyllis Battelle reports that the average savings in all American households today is $7,300. If you have anywhere near this much in savings, shop around to find the bank that pays the highest rate of interest. Savings and Loan Associations usually pay a higher rate of interest than others.

You are allowed $100 in tax free income in dividends from stock. (If you are filing a joint return, both you and your husband must have interest or dividends amounting to $100; one cannot have $200, the other, none.) Your first stocks in your portfolio should be dividend-producing stocks, so that you can take advantage of the allowed deduction.

Other free money sources

If you build an all electric Gold Medallion home (or convert to one) your local electric company will pay you for permission to show your home to builders, contractors or electricians on a given afternoon. (Our check was for $175 when we converted our barn to an all electric home.)

If you own woodland, the Soil Conservation people will pay *you* to clear your own land or improve it in line with good forestry and conservation practices, maximum payment per acre $45.

The best money you will ever receive is money that comes to you after you think you have been "taken." If you feel that you have been misused by a lawyer, write to the Grievance Committee which is located nearest to you; by a real estate broker, to the State Insurance Commission at the State House; for suspected malpractice of a physician or a dentist, to the head of your local medical association or dental society, and ask where to report the case. If your case is a good one, you will receive a rebate.

For restitution for a fraud (a car has 42,000 miles on it which a used car dealer conceals) write to your state's Bureau of Consumer Fraud or to your Better Business Bureau.

3

"Class Distinction Is a Matter of Taste"

You may not agree with Karl Marx's views on capitalism, but you can see the sense in his observation above. The common denominator in any group is taste which Webster defines as *"the ability to appreciate excellence."*

Social climbers who try to break into a group where the appreciation of excellence is a notch above their own are doomed to failure. Almost unconsciously a hostess makes out a guest list of persons with like tastes.

"Good God! Woman!" says the King to the Queen in a recent Modell cartoon, "What's wrong with the crown you have!"

Well might he wonder. Americans senselessly overspend to impress themselves and others. Only if their purchases reflect an ever-improving taste will these purchases give them satisfaction.

Five-step plan for improving your taste

Whether you are 19, 39 or 79, you can improve your taste by following this simple plan.

1. *Forget the Joneses*
   Ask yourself one question when you buy, "Does this please me?" Forget what others may think, and rely on your own judgment. You may make mistakes but you will profit from them.

2. *Depend on your innate awareness of beauty*
A child reacts to *natural* beauty instinctively. Once you rid yourself of the habit of looking at the world through the eyes of others, you will find that the taste you were born with is better than you know.

3. *Search for the real; skip the imitation*
Buy real leather, real silk, real wood, whenever you can. Get fewer possessions but good ones. Get a few table settings of sterling for small dinner parties rather than 12 of everything in silver plate. Get a real leather bag rather than three imitation bags. Get one real diamond rather than a drawer full of fake stones.

4. *Study the masters*
"Every time anyone gets excited about a new book," said our neighbor, "I read an old one." He wastes no time with anything that has not stood the test of time. Until you gain confidence in your own taste, turn to the books and the plays and the art and the music which have stood the test of time. Ask your local librarian to give you a list of the 100 best books ever written. Read one that looks appealing, then another, and another. Go to museums. Look at paintings and sculpture that have lived for centuries. Listen to the classics of music as you do things at home.

5. *Know what products are made in what countries*
Your taste will improve as you learn to recognize work done by the ablest craftsmen in the world.

Follow these rules and the quality of the purchases you make will improve. As you gain in self-reliance, you will spend less money for good merchandise than you once spent for inferior things. The merchandise you buy will last longer.

And about the Joneses. You can forget about them, because from now on the Joneses will be keeping up with you.

Bibliography

Anthony, Katherine, *Louisa May Alcott*, Alfred Knopf, New York, 1938

Barry, Naomi, *Paris Personal*, E. P. Dutton & Company, Inc., New York, 1963

Baruch, Bernard, *My Own Story*, Henry Holt & Co., 1957

Frommer, Arthur, *Europe on Five Dollars a Day*, Arthur Frommer, Inc., 1957

Gunther, John, *Taken at the Flood*, Harper's, New York, 1960

Heidingsfeld, Myron S. & Blankenship, Albert, *Marketing*, Barnes and Noble, New York, 1959

Margolius, Sydney, *How to Buy More for Your Money*, Doubleday, New York, 1947

Ogilvy, David, *Confessions of an Advertising Man*, Atheneum Press, New York, 1963

Osborn, Robert, *Leisure*, Simon & Schuster, 1956

Porter, Sylvia, *How to Get More for Your Money*, World, 1961

Squire, Elizabeth, *The Mail Order Shopping Guide*, M. Barrows & Company, New York, 1963

Superintendent of Documents, Washington, D.C., *Food for Fitness, a Daily Food Guide*

Weisinger, Mort, *1001 Valuable Things You Can Get Free*, Bantam Books, New York, 1961

Index